Meditations

Marcus Aurelius, Felix R. Buchwald

Contents

Introduction

I n the quiet moments before dawn, a Roman emperor sat with his thoughts, compos-ing reflections and instructions that would resonate through the centuries. These are the Meditations of Marcus Aurelius, timeless wisdom of Stoicism, personal experiences, and the weighty responsibility of leadership. This enduring work has been a source of guidance and comfort for countless individuals seeking solace and strength in a turbulent world.

What sets this edition apart is not only its accessible, smoother language but also its unique interactive component: a series of thoughtfully designed workbook prompts concluding each book. This distinctive feature is the core of this offering, turning the passive act of reading into an active process of self-discovery and personal evolution. These reflective journaling questions are your invitation to pause and ponder, to internalize the wisdom of the text, and to examine your own life through the lens of Aureliuses' philosophy. They encourage a dialogue between Marcus Aurelius' insights and your personal growth, challenging you to apply his teachings to contemporary living.

The Meditations are presented in twelve distinct books, each a collection of Marcus Aurelius' private musings and philosophical contemplations. The structure is not linear but cyclical, with themes revisited and deepened as the emperor reflects on the nature of the universe, the virtues of Stoicism, and the art of living.

What you can expect is a deeply personal account, where the most powerful man in the world humbly confronts his own thoughts and shortcomings. There is no grandstanding here—only a quest for truth and virtue.

As you explore these pages, you will be intrigued by the timeless nature of human concerns—how strikingly the thoughts of a second-century emperor mirror our own. You will engage with ideas on resilience, integrity, and the pursuit of good, finding that the essence of a fulfilled life remains unchanged despite the passing of time.

This book is not just a reading experience; it is a philosophical toolkit for life. It is a companion for those seeking to understand the complexities of their own existence, a guide for those who strive to lead with compassion and wisdom, and a sanctuary for those in search of tranquility amidst chaos.

Welcome to the Meditations of Marcus Aurelius.

Meditations: Book I

From my grandfather Verus, I learned the virtues of good morals and self-control.

The esteemed memory of my father taught me modesty and the essence of a virtuous character.

From my mother, I acquired a spirit of reverence and charity, and the restraint to avoid not just wrongful actions but also harmful intentions; moreover, she instilled in me an appreciation for a life of simplicity, distinctly apart from the extravagances of the wealthy.

My great-grandfather imparted the wisdom of favoring private instruction over public education, the privilege of having capable teachers within my own home, and the understanding that such education merits generous investment.

From my governor, I learned not to align myself with any particular faction at the chariot races, be it the team of the Greens or the Blues, nor to side with the shield-bearing gladiators over those who fought with the sword; from him, I also gained the virtues of hard work, frugality, and self-reliance, and the principles of non-interference in the matters of others and to avoid indulging in gossip.

From Diognetus, I was taught to disregard trivial pursuits and to be skeptical of the claims made by sorcerers and charlatans about spells and exorcising demons; not to engage in rearing fighting quails, nor to become excessively attached to such distractions; and to tolerate outspokenness. I was introduced to philosophy, attended lectures by Bacchius, followed by Tandasis and Marcianus; in my younger years, I composed dialogues, aspired to the simplicity of a wooden bed and a mere skin for cover, and embraced the other aspects that are characteristic of Greek discipline.

From Rusticus, I adopted the understanding that my character needed refinement and control. He taught me not to be swayed into empty debates or to engage in abstract theorizing, not to give minor motivational talks, nor to parade myself as a man of excessive self-discipline or one who performs acts of kindness merely for show. He advised me to avoid grandiloquence, poetry, and elaborate writing; to not wear my outdoor garments indoors; and other such vanities. He instructed me to compose my letters plainly, emulating the straightforward style of the letter Rusticus sent my mother from Sinuessa. He instilled in me the grace to forgive and seek reconciliation with those who have insulted or wronged me, once they exhibit a willingness to make amends; to study texts diligently, avoiding a shallow grasp of their content; not to readily agree with those who speak too much; and I owe to him my familiarity with the lectures of Epictetus, which he shared from his own collection.

From Apollonius, I absorbed the essence of free will and unwavering commitment to my objectives; to dedicate myself solely to the dictates of reason, unswayed by any distraction; and to maintain a consistent demeanor through severe pain, the grief of losing a child, or during prolonged illness. He exemplified the rare combination of firm resolve with a flexible, ungrudging approach to teaching. He regarded his vast experience and ability to elucidate philosophical concepts as the least of his strengths. From him, I also learned to accept kindnesses from friends graciously, without feeling demeaned or failing to acknowledge them.

From Sextus, I learned kindness, the image of a household managed with paternal care, and the concept of living in harmony with nature. He exemplified seriousness without pretense and showed meticulous concern for the welfare of friends, tolerating those who were uninformed or who judged hastily. His presence was more pleasant than flattery, yet he commanded immense respect from his peers. He adeptly identified and systematically arranged the principles essential for life. He never succumbed to anger or any passion, was completely free from such disturbances, yet he was deeply compassionate. He could commend without fanfare and was knowledgeable without vanity.

From Alexander the grammarian, I acquired the lesson of refraining from criticism, to gently correct those who use improper language not with reprimand but by subtly introducing the correct phrase within the context of my response or discussion, focusing on the subject matter rather than the incorrect usage, thus guiding without embarrassing them.

From Fronto, I discerned how to recognize the hallmarks of jealousy, deceit, and pretense in a ruler, and to understand that those among us of noble rank often lack the warmth of familial love.

From Alexander the Platonic, I understood the importance of not frequently or unnecessarily telling others or writing in correspondence that I am too busy; nor to habitually use pressing engagements as an excuse for neglecting the responsibilities that come with our relationships to those we are connected with.

From Catulus, I learned the value of not dismissing criticisms from a friend, even if they may be unfounded, but rather to attempt to bring them back to their usual state of mind; and to be ready to commend my educators, as exemplified by Domitius and Athenodotus; and to hold genuine love for my children.

From my brother Severus, I learned to cherish my family, to hold truth in high regard, and to value justice. Through his influence, I became familiar with the virtues of esteemed figures like Thrasea, Helvidius, Cato, Dion, and Brutus. He imparted to me the vision of a republic governed by universal laws, one that upholds equal rights and free speech, and the concept of a sovereign rule that places the liberty of its people above all else. From him, I also learned to be steadfast and unwavering in my dedication to philosophy; to be generous in doing good for others; to maintain optimism; and to trust in the affection of my friends. In Severus, I witnessed a transparency in his judgments about those he disapproved of, ensuring that his friends never had to guess his desires or objections, for they were clearly expressed.

From Maximus, I mastered the art of self-control and the resolve not to be distracted by trivialities. I learned to maintain a spirit of cheerfulness in every situation, including during times of illness. He taught me the balance of gentleness and gravitas in one's

He embodied the adage attributed to Socrates: possessing the strength to both forgo and savor those pleasures that overwhelm the willpower of many. Where others falter and indulge excessively, he demonstrated the capacity to refrain and enjoy in moderation. His self-control and temperance were particularly evident during Maximus's sickness, where he manifested the attributes of a soul that is complete and unconquerable.

I am deeply grateful to the divine for the gift of honorable grandfathers, loving parents, a caring sister, wise teachers, supportive colleagues, loyal relatives, and steadfast friends—essentially, for all the good in my life. Moreover, I am thankful that I was never rushed into wrongdoing against them, despite having a nature that might have been prone to such faults under different circumstances; by the grace of the gods, no such challenging situations arose to test me.

I am also thankful that my time under the guardianship of my grandfather's consort was brief, allowing me to maintain my youthful integrity, and that I chose to delay the exploration of my manhood until it was fitting. I am indebted to the example of a sovereign and a father who humbled me and showed me that one can dwell in grandeur without the lust for guards, luxurious attire, or the ostentatious display of wealth; he taught me that a man might live with the simplicity of a private citizen, without compromising his thoughts or his actions, especially in matters of public welfare, as is expected of a leader.

I am thankful to the gods for bestowing upon me a brother whose virtue inspired my own self-discipline and whose respect and love brought me joy. Gratitude also for my children, who are neither lacking in intellect nor afflicted in form. I am relieved that my talents did not overly advance in rhetoric, poetry, and other pursuits, for I might have become ensnared by them had I excelled.

I am grateful that I promptly honored my mentors with the recognition they desired rather than delaying it, recognizing their youth. I cherish having known Apollonius, Rusticus, Maximus, and for the vivid and recurring insights they provided about living in harmony with nature, which shaped my life's path—though I acknowledge my shortcomings in heeding the gods' guidance and my own failures.

I am thankful that my physical strength has supported me in this lifestyle; that I avoided indiscretions with Benedicta and Theodotus and overcame youthful infatuations. Even when I was displeased with Rusticus, I have no actions to regret. Despite the sorrow of my mother's early passing, I am consoled that she lived her final years with me. Whenever I sought to aid someone in need, I was never hindered by lack of means, nor have I been compelled to rely on others for support.

I am blessed with a wife who is devoted, loving, and of simple grace; fortunate to have found excellent tutors for my children; and grateful for the divine revelations in dreams that offered remedies for ailments and guidance. Lastly, when my interest turned to philosophy, I am thankful that I did not succumb to the sophistry of charlatans, nor did I squander my time on historical writers, logical puzzles, or astrological speculations—all my pursuits guided by the benevolence of the gods and fortune.

Workbook Exercises
Book I

Who influenced you?

Marcus Aurelius begins his meditations with a series of thanks to those who have influenced him. Write a journal entry about the people who have significantly influenced your life and character. For each person, describe what they taught you and how you can continue to apply these lessons in your daily life.

Teachers and Lessons

Marcus was thankful for his teachers. Think about a teacher who has had a significant impact on your life. What did they teach you that still resonates with you now?

Avoiding Negative Traits

Marcus learned not only what to do from others but also what not to do. Reflect on the behaviors you have observed in others that you want to avoid. How do you plan to steer clear of these traits?

Moral Compass

Marcus was influenced by the moral compass of those around him. What guides your moral decisions? How do you ensure you stay true to your principles?

Self-Reflection

Marcus used reflection to better himself. Reflect on an aspect of your character that you're working to improve. What progress have you made, and what challenges do you face?

Meditations: Book II

S tart your day with this reminder: Today, I will encounter the meddlesome, the ungrateful, the arrogant, the deceitful, the envious, and the antisocial. These traits arise from their ignorance of the distinction between good and evil. Having recognized the beauty of goodness and the ugliness of evil, and understanding that the wrongdoer is akin to me—not only sharing ancestry but also a part of the same intelligence and divine essence—I cannot be harmed by them, for ugliness cannot be attributed to me. Nor can I feel anger towards my relative or disdain them. We are designed to work together, like parts of the body—feet, hands, eyelids, or the aligned rows of teeth. To work against each other is against our nature; irritation and aversion are forms of such conflict.

As for what I am, it is merely flesh, breath, and the governing spirit. Put aside your books; do not distract yourself further—it is not permissible. Instead, as if you were on the verge of death, regard the body with indifference: it is mere flesh, bones, a lattice of nerves, veins, and arteries. Consider breath as well: it is nothing but air, constantly expelled and drawn back in. The vital element is the governing spirit. Reflect on this: You are advanced in years; it is time to free your spirit from servitude, to stop being jerked about like a puppet on strings by unsociable impulses, and to be neither discontent with your current circumstances nor fearful of the future.

Everything that comes from the gods is infused with providence. Even what we attribute to chance is not disconnected from nature or the weave of fate orchestrated by providence. From this source all things originate, and within it lies both destiny and the benefit of the universe, of which you are an integral part. What is beneficial for each part of nature is that which sustains and supports the nature of the whole. The preservation of the universe is achieved through the transformation of the elements and the things they compose. Let these truths be fundamental to you and hold them as constant beliefs. Yet, dismiss your craving for more books, so that you may not meet your end in frustration, but in gladness, with sincerity and gratitude to the gods in your heart.

Be mindful of how much time you have already let slip by, and how many times the gods have afforded you the chance for reflection, yet you have not embraced it. It is time to realize the vastness of the cosmos to which you belong, and the divine principle from which your life flows. Understand that your time is limited; if you do not use it to dispel the fog from your mind, it will pass, and you with it, never to return.

Consistently remind yourself to think and act with the steadfastness of a Roman, with the integrity of a man, focused on the task at hand with unadorned dignity, warmth, freedom, and fairness; and by doing so, liberate yourself from all other distractions. You will find this liberation if you perform every action as if it were your last, casting away negligence, resistance to reason, pretense, self-centeredness, and dissatisfaction with your lot in life. Notice how few are the necessities for a life of tranquility, similar to that of the gods; and for such a life, the gods demand nothing more from the one who practices these principles.

You are doing harm to yourself, my soul, if you do not honor your own worth. The opportunity to esteem yourself is fleeting. A single lifetime is enough for those who manage it well; and yours is nearing its end, yet you fail to honor your own spirit, seeking instead your happiness in the esteem of others.

Do external events disrupt your peace? Allow yourself time to learn something worthwhile and cease to spin in a whirlwind. But be careful not to be swept in the opposite direction either. There are those who have exhausted themselves with busyness in life yet have no clear purpose for their actions or thoughts.

Rarely has a person become unhappy by not understanding someone else's thoughts; but those who do not reflect upon the workings of their own minds are bound to be unhappy.

Always keep in mind the nature of the universe and your own nature, and how your part relates to the whole—what role you play within the vastness. Remember that nothing can prevent you from acting and speaking in harmony with the nature of which you are a part.

Theophrastus, in his discussions of moral failings, compares them based on general human attitudes and asserts, with philosophical rigor, that transgressions born of desire are more reprehensible than those arising from anger. He suggests that one overtaken by anger seems to reject reason with a kind of distress and unthinking tension; whereas one who sins from desire, succumbing to pleasure, appears to be more uncontrolled and shows a lack of restraint that could be seen as more disgraceful. Therefore, philosophically and justly, he claims that a misdeed committed with enjoyment is more culpable than one committed with discomfort; and broadly speaking, the former resembles someone acting out of a flawed impulse to do wrong, driven by desire, while the latter is like someone reacting with indignation due to being wronged and thus driven to anger.

Recognize that you could leave this life at any moment; therefore, guide every action and thought with that awareness. If you were to depart from the company of men and gods exist, there is no reason to fear, for the gods will not subject you to harm. If gods do not exist, or if they pay no mind to human affairs, then what concern is it of mine to live in a universe empty of gods or divine foresight? However, the truth is that gods do exist and they are concerned with human affairs, providing us with the resources necessary to avoid true misfortune. If there were any real evils, they would have ensured that we could completely avoid them. What does not damage a person's character cannot damage their life. It is inconceivable that the universe, through oversight, ignorance, or impotence, has failed to address these issues; nor has it erred so grievously that good and evil befall both the just and unjust without distinction. Death and life, honor and dishonor, pain and pleasure befall both virtuous and vicious alike, and since they do not improve or degrade our character, they are neither good nor evil in themselves.

To witness the fleeting nature of all things is a task for the mind: how even the bodies within the universe vanish, and in time, even the memory of them fades. Consider the essence of all tangible things, especially those that lure with the promise of pleasure or alarm with the threat of pain, or those acclaimed by transient fame—how trivial, contemptible, base, ephemeral, and lifeless they are. The mind should note these things. It should also consider the nature of those whose approval and words confer fame; what death truly is—that if a person contemplates it on its own terms, breaking down by rational thought all that seems fearsome about it, he will understand that it is nothing more than a natural process. And to fear a natural process is to be like a child. Yet this process is not just natural; it is also conducive to the workings of nature. It is also part of the mind's work to observe how a human being can approach divinity, through which part of himself, and under what conditions this aspect of a person aligns with the divine.

There is no greater misery than that of the man who circles endlessly, exploring all things below the heavens—as the poet claims—and who probes the thoughts of those around him, not realizing that it is enough to tend to the spirit within and to honor it truly. Honoring the spirit means keeping it untouched by intense emotion, thoughtlessness, and discontent with what is given by the gods and by men. What comes from the gods should be held in awe for its perfection; and what comes from men should be cherished for our common humanity. At times, it should even evoke our compassion, considering their inability to discern good from bad—a shortcoming as grave as the inability to distinguish between white and black.

Whether you are destined to live for three thousand years, or times ten thousand, bear in mind that no one can lose any life other than the one he is living now, nor can he live any life other than the one he is losing right now. The greatest and the smallest life spans are equal in this sense: the present moment is the same for all, yet what is gone is not the same; hence, what is lost seems to be just a fleeting instant. For how can someone be deprived of the past or the future? If something is not in one's possession, it cannot be taken away. Remember two things: first, that all things from the beginning are of similar forms and they cycle in a circle, and it makes no difference whether a man witnesses the same events for a hundred or two hundred years, or for an eternity; and second, that he who has the longest life to live and he who will depart soonest will lose the same thing: the present, for that is all a man truly owns, and one cannot lose something that one never had.

It's crucial to understand that everything is a matter of perspective. The sayings of the Cynic philosopher Monimus are clear, and so is their value, provided one interprets them to extract the truth within.

The soul inflicts harm upon itself first when it becomes inflamed with discontent, swelling like a sore on the world, which it is inherently a part of. To resent what happens is to detach oneself from nature, despite being embedded within the same fabric that encompasses all beings. Secondly, the soul harms itself when it shuns or seeks to harm others, embodying the bitterness of those consumed by anger. Thirdly, the soul is damaged when it succumbs to pleasure or pain. Fourthly, it is harmed when it is not authentic, when it acts or speaks with insincerity and falsehood. Lastly, the soul is violated when it acts aimlessly, without thoughtful consideration, even in trivial matters, for it is essential that all actions, no matter how small, are directed towards a purpose. The ultimate purpose for rational beings is to adhere to reason and to the laws of the oldest society and government.

The essence of human life is ephemeral: our time is but a fleeting moment, our physical substance is ever-changing, our senses are limited, our bodies are destined to decay, the soul is a restless eddy, fortune is enigmatic, and reputation is often misjudged. To sum it up, all that is of the body flows like a river, all that is of the soul is ephemeral, life is akin to a battle and a visit in a land not our own, and the legacy we leave behind will eventually fade into obscurity.

What, then, can guide a person through such a transient existence? There is but one answer: philosophy. True philosophy involves maintaining the inner spirit in a state of tranquility, untouched by affliction or excess, independent of pleasure or pain. It calls for deliberate action, free of deceit or insincerity, without reliance on the actions of others. It requires embracing whatever comes our way, whatever is our lot, as emanating from the same source we ourselves originate from. And at the journey's end, it teaches us to face death with equanimity, recognizing it as merely the separation and transformation of the elements that constitute all living entities. If there is no inherent damage to these elements as they transform one into another, then there should be no fear for their combination's dissolution. For it is the way of nature, and there is no malice in that which is natural.

Workbook Exercises
Book II

Nature's Intention

Marcus speaks of acting in accordance with nature. Reflect on what 'acting according to nature' means to you. How do you interpret this in the context of your daily life?

Reaction to Obstacles

Marcus suggests that what stands in the way becomes the way. Write about a recent obstacle you've faced and how you can, or have, turned it into an opportunity for growth.

Dealing with Difficult People

Marcus advises us on how to deal with those who wrong us. Recall a recent interaction with a difficult person and explore how you can apply Marcus' advice to manage such situations with equanimity.

The Present Moment

Reflect on the importance of living fully in the present moment. Are there areas in your life where you find this particularly challenging? How can you improve your focus on the here and now?

Universal Connectedness

Reflect on the idea that we are all parts of a larger whole. How does this perspective influence your interactions with others and your sense of social responsibility?

Meditations: Book III

As we navigate the passage of time, it's not just the diminishing span of our lives we must acknowledge, but also the uncertainty that comes with age — the question of whether our minds will retain the capacity to grasp and contemplate the fundamental truths of the divine and the human. The functions of the body may persist: breathing, eating, sensory perception, desires, and all similar aspects may continue unabated. However, the ability to exercise our rational faculties, to fulfill our moral obligations, to discern reality clearly, to contemplate our mortality, and to engage in the kind of rigorous reasoning that a disciplined mind can undertake — these are the faculties that may wane first.

Thus, the urgency to act, to learn, and to understand is not only propelled by our inevitable approach towards death but also by the potential decline in our mental acuity. The clarity of thought and the power of introspection may begin to dim even as the body's more basic functions march on. It is this potential eclipse of the understanding, even before life itself wanes, that must spur us to haste in our pursuit of wisdom and virtue.

We should also take note that even the occurrences that ensue from the natural course of things hold their own allure and charm. For instance, during the baking of bread, some parts may crack open on the surface. These spontaneous openings, which deviate from the baker's intended design, possess a unique beauty and kindle an appetite within us. Similarly, figs, when fully ripe, split open; and it is precisely the state of being on the verge of spoilage that bestows a distinctive beauty upon ripe olives.

The drooping heads of grain, the furrowed brows of lions, the froth on the muzzles of wild boars, among many other sights—while not conventionally beautiful when viewed in isolation—nevertheless enhance the natural world and delight the mind. This is because they arise from nature's own processes. Anyone who cultivates a deep appreciation and understanding of the universe will find beauty in these natural consequences. Such a person can observe with equal pleasure the open maws of wild creatures as those replicated by artists, perceive a dignified elegance in the aged, and regard the youthful allure with pure appreciation. These experiences are not universally pleasing but are reserved for those who have grown deeply acquainted with nature and her workings.

Hippocrates, despite healing many illnesses, eventually succumbed to his own and passed away. The Chaldeans, who predicted the demise of many, were themselves seized by death. Great figures like Alexander, Pompey, and Julius Caesar, who razed cities and slaughtered legions, also met their own ends. Heraclitus, who pondered over the universe's fiery end, was ironically taken by a buildup of fluid within him, dying covered in mud. Democritus was consumed by vermin; even Socrates fell to a similar fate. What do these tales tell us? You have set sail, completed your journey, and now you've reached the shore; it's time to disembark. If there's another life awaiting, the gods will abound there too. But if you're to enter a state devoid of sensation, you'll be released from the grip of pain and pleasure, no longer enslaved to the body, which is far inferior to the soul that serves it. For the soul is akin to intelligence and divinity, while the body is mere earth and decay.

Do not squander the time you have left on earth with preoccupations about others, unless your considerations contribute to the common good. Engaging in such thoughts, wondering what someone else is doing, saying, thinking, or planning, distracts from self-regulation and wastes time that could be used productively. We should eliminate all aimless and unproductive thoughts, especially those of an overly curious or harmful nature. Strive to maintain thoughts that you could readily disclose if asked suddenly; thoughts that demonstrate clarity, kindness, and alignment with the nature of a social being—one that doesn't obsess over pleasures, engage in competition, or harbor envy and suspicion. In essence, keep your mind such that you would never hesitate to reveal its contents, for they are nothing but straightforward and good-natured.

For the individual who aspires to be among the best and no longer postpones this quest, he resembles a sacred servant of the divine, harnessing the inner godlike nature within him. This inner divinity renders him untainted by pleasure, unscathed by pain, impervious to insult, and immune to injury. He engages in the most honorable struggle, not swayed by base passions, steeped in righteousness, embracing his fate with his whole being; and he seldom, and only when absolutely necessary for the common good, concerns himself with the words, actions, or thoughts of others. He focuses solely on what is within his own sphere of influence, ensuring his actions are honorable and convinced of the goodness of his own share in life. He understands that his destiny is intertwined with him, propelling him forward. He is mindful that every rational being is kin, and that caring for humanity aligns with human nature. He values the opinions not of everyone, but of those who openly adhere to nature's principles. Regarding those who do not live by these principles, he is aware of their true nature, their private and public behaviors, their nocturnal and diurnal habits, and the tainted company they keep. Thus, he does not regard the commendations from such individuals, for they do not even meet their own standards of self-satisfaction.

Embrace your duties with a spirit of willingness, aligned with the greater good, and thoughtful consideration, without getting scattered or distracted. Eschew superfluous embellishment in your thoughts; be neither overly verbose nor overly engaged in numerous tasks. Let your inner divinity be the custodian of a living being who is mature, virtuous, involved in civic duties, a citizen of Rome, and a leader. Stand prepared, like a soldier at his post, ready for the signal to depart from life, requiring no pledge or witness to affirm your readiness. Maintain a cheerful disposition, and do not rely on external assistance or the peace provided by others. You must hold yourself upright through your own strength, not depending on others to uphold you.

If you discover anything in life more virtuous than integrity, truthfulness, self-control, bravery, or essentially, anything superior to the contentment of your own conscience in acting justly and reasonably within the circumstances you did not choose—if you find something better, pursue it wholeheartedly and relish what you have determined to be supreme. However, if you deem nothing higher than your inner divinity, which governs your desires and scrutinizes all perceptions, and as Socrates professed, has emancipated itself from the deceptions of the senses, has aligned with the divine, and is attentive to humanity—if all else seems inferior to this, yield to nothing else. If you deviate and give in to other allurements, you will lose focus and fail to prioritize the true good that is inherently yours; no external approval, authority, or sensual delight should rival what is intellectually and morally excellent. Even if they appear to contribute modestly to the greater good, they can quickly dominate and sway us. Thus, choose the superior path with simplicity and conviction. If it is beneficial to you as a rational being, adhere to it; if only beneficial to your basic instincts, acknowledge it, but keep your discernment intact and without pretension. Ensure that your evaluation is grounded in a reliable and rational approach.

Do not consider anything beneficial if it requires you to break a promise, compromise your dignity, foster hatred, engage in suspicion or cursing, or be deceitful. Desires that necessitate privacy and secrecy should not be valued. One who prioritizes wisdom, the guiding spirit within, and the pursuit of its excellence does not engage in drama, nor laments or requires isolation or extensive company. Importantly, such a person lives indifferent to the duration of life, not chasing nor avoiding death, but remains as composed in facing mortality as in undertaking any other dignified and orderly task. Throughout life, their focus remains on maintaining the integrity of an intelligent being and a responsible member of society.

In the heart of a person who is disciplined and pure, you will not find decay, impurity, or superficial wounds. Their life is not considered incomplete if it ends prematurely, just as an actor's performance is not lessened if they exit before the play concludes. There is nothing servile, pretentious, overly dependent, or detached in their nature, nothing deserving of reproach, and nothing that seeks concealment.

Honor the capacity to form opinions, for it is this power that determines whether your ruling mind harbors any belief that contradicts the nature of a rational being. This ability ensures that we avoid rash judgments, promotes goodwill towards others, and fosters compliance with divine will.

Discard all else and cleave to only a few essential principles; also, remember that each person only truly possesses the present moment—a fleeting and indivisible point in time. All other parts of life are either already gone or remain uncertain. Thus, the span of life granted to each individual is brief, and the piece of earth they inhabit is just a tiny fragment. Even the fame that survives after one's death is short-lived, carried on by a chain of fragile humans who are themselves close to death and who have little understanding of themselves, much less of someone who passed away long ago.

Augment your existing supports with this: Craft a clear definition or description of what is before you, to fully perceive its essence, its raw form, and its entirety. Name it accurately, as well as the components it is made of and what it will eventually decompose into. There is no greater mental uplift than to be able to systematically and truthfully scrutinize each object that life presents, while also considering the nature of the universe it belongs to, its role within it, its significance in relation to the entirety and to humanity—humanity which resides in the greatest of cities, where other cities are mere districts. Understand what a thing truly is, what constitutes it, and how long it is destined to make an impression on you. Recognize what virtues are necessary to engage with it appropriately, such as kindness, bravery, honesty, loyalty, straightforwardness, satisfaction, and others. Hence, a person should acknowledge on every occasion: this is of divine origin; this aligns with fate's distribution and the weaving of destiny; this is fortuitous or coincidental; and this originates from one who is of the same blood, a relative and ally, yet unaware of his nature. But I am aware; thus, I act towards him in a manner consistent with the natural laws of community, with goodwill and fairness. Meanwhile, for matters of neutral consequence, I strive to discern the worth of each.

Engage diligently with your current tasks, guided by sound reasoning, with earnestness, vitality, and tranquility, allowing no diversions, maintaining the sanctity of your inner spirit as if it were to be returned forthwith. Clinging to this ethos—anticipating nothing, dreading nothing, content in the natural course of your actions, speaking and expressing with noble honesty—you shall find contentment. And no one has the power to impede this state of happiness.

Just as a surgeon keeps scalpels and instruments at the ready for urgent medical needs, you too should prepare your principles to comprehend the divine and the human realms, and to perform all acts, even the most trivial, with mindfulness of the tie that links divinity with humanity. For you cannot excel in human endeavors without heeding the divine, nor can you manage divine matters without considering the human aspect.

Cease your aimless meandering; the time for reading your memoirs or the chronicles of ancient Rome and Greece, and the literary treasures you've been saving for your twilight years, will not come. So hasten towards your destined conclusion, and cast aside vain aspirations. Assist yourself, if you have any regard for your own well-being, while you still wield the capability.

Many fail to understand the depth of actions implied by terms like stealing, sowing, buying, maintaining silence, and recognizing one's duties; for such comprehension does not come from the mere function of sight, but through a different kind of vision, an inner discernment.

Body, soul, and intelligence: these are the realms of sensation, desire, and principles, respectively. Sensation is a faculty shared even by the beasts, drawing in the world through appearances. Desire can enslave all creatures, be they wild beasts or men who have surrendered their strength, akin to the tyrants Phalaris and Nero. Intelligence, the ability to discern what seems fitting, is not unique either, found even in those who deny the gods, betray their country, or commit vile acts behind closed doors.

However, among these common faculties, there is one that remains the exclusive domain of the virtuous: to accept and be content with the unfolding of fate, to honor the divine spark within without sullying it with a tumult of images, but to keep it serene, to follow it as one would a deity, speaking only truth, acting justly. And should all refuse to acknowledge his integrity and contentedness, he harbors no resentment, nor does he stray from the path that leads to life's natural end—a path he treads pure, calm, willing, in harmony with his fate.

Workbook Excercises
Book III

A uthenticity and Self-Examination

Marcus urges us to remove the masks and face ourselves truly. Reflect on what aspects of your 'mask' you present to the world. How can you live more authentically?

Acceptance of Life's Events

Marcus advises acceptance of what life brings as if you had chosen it. Reflect on an event you initially resisted. How might embracing it as if you had chosen it change your perspective?

Living Purposefully

Marcus emphasizes doing everything with purpose. Reflect on your daily routines. Are there actions you perform without purpose? How can you imbue them with intention?

Inner Contentment

Reflect on Marcus' suggestion to find contentment within rather than in external validation. How do you seek approval from others, and how can you cultivate a greater sense of internal contentment?

Facing Mortality

Marcus often contemplates mortality. Reflect on how the awareness of your mortality influences the choices you make and the life you lead.

Meditations: Book IV

T he innermost ruling part, when aligned with nature, interacts with life's events in such a manner that it seamlessly conforms to reality as it presents itself. This inner guide is not reliant on specific circumstances to operate; instead, it purposefully navigates through them. It can transform adversities into fuel, much like a robust fire that seizes upon whatever is thrown into it. A small flame might flicker and die when overwhelmed, but a mighty blaze will use the same challenge to grow even stronger, ascending higher as it consumes the material that once threatened to smother it.

From this metaphor, we draw a lesson for our actions: let them all be purposeful, not haphazard. They should conform to the highest standards of excellence, as if each were a work of art crafted by following the utmost principles of mastery. Each deed should reflect a deliberate intent and adhere to the refined skills of one's craft.

People often seek peace and solitude in physical spaces—homes tucked away in the countryside, the serenity of the seaside, the solitude of the mountains. You, too, have longed for such sanctuaries. However, such desires are common and miss an essential truth: you can retreat into your own mind at any moment. The quietest and most peaceful refuge can be found within your own soul, especially when it contains thoughts that can summon a state of serenity instantaneously. True tranquility is the result of a well-ordered mind.

Make it a practice to retreat into this inner sanctuary frequently, to refresh yourself. Your guiding principles should be concise and fundamental, capable of purifying the soul and restoring you to a state of contentment with the world you engage with. If you find yourself discontented, what is the cause? Is it the misdeeds of others? Remember then, that rational beings are meant to coexist, that patience is a virtue of justice, and that wrongdoing is often not out of malice but ignorance.

Reflect on the many who have perished in conflict and contention, who now lie still, their disputes long settled in the silence of oblivion. Let this contemplation guide you towards peace.

If you're feeling discontent with your lot in the cosmos, consider this dichotomy: either there is a guiding providence or there is a random collision of atoms. Reflect on the arguments that support the notion of the universe as a political community, and let this thought bring you to a place of acceptance.

If physical sensations still cling to you, delve deeper. Remember that the mind can remain unaffected by the body's sensations when it understands its own strength. Recall what you have accepted as true about pain and pleasure, and find your peace in that knowledge.

And if you are haunted by a desire for fame, consider the fleeting nature of renown. Observe the vast expanse of time that stretches endlessly before and after the present moment, and the futility of praise. Praise is often given without true discernment, and its existence is limited to a tiny stage in the vast theater of eternity.

Finally, consider the insignificance of the Earth within the vast universe, and within it, the even smaller space that you inhabit. Think of the limited number of people who know you and those who might offer praise. Recognizing the limited scope and duration of fame and acclaim should bring you tranquility. The quest for external validation is dwarfed by the scale of the universe and the transitory nature of human affairs. Embrace this perspective, and find your rest in it.

The essence of tranquility lies within, in that personal domain that belongs only to you. It's crucial to remember not to exhaust or distract yourself, but to maintain your freedom and view life through the lenses of humanity and mortality.

Two fundamental truths should always be at your immediate disposal for contemplation. First, external events cannot disturb the soul; they are immutable in their essence.
It is only our internal judgments that cause unrest. Second, all that you observe around
you is in a state of constant flux, and it will soon transform into something else. Reflect
on the multitude of changes you have already experienced in your life.

The cosmos is in a perpetual state of metamorphosis, and what we perceive as life is
merely a series of perceptions. By internalizing these concepts, you can cultivate a serene
state of mind that remains undisturbed by external circumstances and steadfast through
the incessant changes of life.

Your reflection navigates the profound interconnectedness of human beings through
our shared capacity for reason. If we accept that our intellectual abilities are universal,
then the logic that guides our actions is also a shared attribute. This implies a collective
reasoning behind our choices of what to do and what not to do, suggesting the existence
of a universal law that binds us together.

If we follow this line of thought, we are more than just random inhabitants of the
Earth; we are, in a deep sense, fellow citizens of a global community. This leads to the
vision of the world as a single, unified state encompassing all humanity. Just as our physical
components are derived from the elements of the Earth, our intellectual and reasoning
capabilities must originate from a common source as well.

This perspective invites us to view each individual as part of a larger, more complex
organism — humanity itself — with each person contributing to the collective consciousness and society. It's a powerful reminder of our shared human experience and the
innate laws that govern not only our individual existence but also our interactions with
one another on a global scale.

Death is akin to birth, a profound mystery of the natural world. It involves a formation
from the same elements and a return to them. Such a process should not be a source
of shame for anyone, as it is not at odds with the nature of a rational being or the
fundamental logic of our existence.

The actions of certain individuals are to be expected as part of the necessary order of things. To resist these natural processes is as futile as denying the fig tree its sap. Keep in mind that it won't be long before you and those individuals will have passed away, and even the memory of your names will fade into oblivion.

If you dismiss your belief that you have been wronged, then the sense of grievance disappears. Without the grievance, the sense of injury also vanishes.

An event that does not diminish a person's virtue does not worsen their life or cause them true harm, whether from external sources or from within.

The essence of what is beneficial by universal standards is inherently bound to act in such a way.

Reflect on the idea that all events unfold justly, and with close observation, you will see that this is true. I refer not only to the natural order of events but also to their inherent fairness, as though they were determined by a judicious force that assigns each event its proper value. Continue this awareness as you have started; and align every act you undertake with the essence of goodness, in the truest sense of what it means to be a virtuous person. Commit to this principle in all your endeavors.

Do not adopt the perspective of those who wrong you, or the perspective they would prefer you to have, but see things as they actually are.

Keep these two guiding principles at hand: first, act only according to the dictates of reason, the part of you that governs and creates laws for the benefit of humankind; second, be willing to revise your beliefs if someone corrects you and prompts you to abandon an erroneous view. However, let such a change in perspective be driven by genuine conviction—whether it concerns fairness, the common good, or similar considerations—not by the prospect of pleasure or the desire for approval.

Do you possess the faculty of reason? Yes, you do. Then why do you not employ it? For if it functions as it should, what more could you desire?

You have been a part of the whole. You will dissolve back into the source that created you; but more accurately, you will be transformed back into its originating essence.

Countless granules of incense are placed upon the same altar: one may drop sooner, another later; but in the end, the sequence is inconsequential.

In a mere ten days, you could be revered as divine by those who currently see you as nothing more than a wild animal or a primitive creature, if only you return to your fundamental principles and the veneration of rational thought.

Do not live as if you have ten thousand years left. Death looms over you. While you live and have the agency to do so, choose to be virtuous.

Consider how much strife one avoids by not concerning oneself with the words, actions, or thoughts of others, but focusing solely on one's own actions to ensure they are righteous and pure. Or, as Agathon suggests, do not glance at the corrupt behaviors of others, but proceed straightforwardly on your path without straying.

One who craves lasting fame fails to realize that those who remember him will also soon pass away; and in turn, so will their successors, until memory itself is extinguished, passed on by mortal men who in their folly, admire and then fade away. But even if those who remember were to live forever, and the memory were to be eternal, what significance would that hold for you? And I do not ask what it means for the deceased, but for the living. What is praise but merely useful to a certain extent? You now unwisely forsake nature's gift, grasping instead for something more...

Beauty, in any form, exists in and of itself and ends with itself. It does not become part of its essence to be praised. A thing is not diminished or enhanced by commendation. This truth applies even to those things deemed beautiful by common standards, such as physical objects and artworks. True beauty requires nothing beyond itself; not any more than laws, truth, kindness, or decency require. Do any of these gain beauty through praise or lose their worth through criticism? Is an emerald any less if it goes unpraised? Or what of gold, ivory, purple dyes, a lyre, a simple knife, a blossom, or a bush?

If souls persist after death, one might wonder how the atmosphere can contain them all through eternity. Similarly, how does the earth accommodate the bodies of those who have been interred for ages? Just as the transformation and decay of bodies over time make space for new ones to be buried, so too might souls, after existing in the air for a while, undergo a change. They might be refined and dispersed, becoming part of the universe's creative force, thereby making room for new souls to enter. This is one way to conceive of the soul's journey, assuming they endure after death.

But consider not only the vast number of bodies laid to rest in the earth but also the multitude of creatures consumed daily by humans and other predators. The sheer quantity that is consumed, and in a sense interred within the bodies of their consumers, is staggering. Yet the earth still has room for them because these bodies are converted into blood, and their matter is transformed into air or fire. This cycle of consumption and transformation allows the earth to continue accommodating new life.

The quest for truth can be seen as a quest to discern the material from the formal, the substance from the blueprint that gives it shape.

Resist being tossed by the tides of circumstance. Instead, let every action be guided by justice, and with every new perception, sustain your ability to understand.

I am in harmony with what aligns with you, Universe. Nothing is too premature or too delayed for me that corresponds with your timing. All that your cycles yield is bountiful to me, Nature, for from you all things emerge, within you all things exist, and into you all things will return. Just as the poet cherishes the city of Cecrops, should we not also cherish the city of Zeus?

The philosopher advises to engage in a limited number of activities to achieve peace of mind. Yet, it may be more beneficial to focus on what is essential and what the rational nature of a social being demands. This approach not only offers the calm that comes from doing good but also from doing less. Most of what we say and do is not necessary; if we eliminate these superfluous actions, we'll find more time and less stress. Therefore, we should constantly question whether our actions and thoughts are necessary, avoiding the unnecessary so that needless actions do not ensue.

Experiment with the lifestyle of a virtuous individual, one who is content with his share of the whole and at peace with his just deeds and kind nature.

Have you observed those things? Then consider these as well. Do not trouble yourself. Embrace simplicity. If someone commits an error, they have wronged themselves. If something has happened to you, remember that from the universe's inception, all events have been distributed and allotted to you. To put it succinctly, your life is fleeting. You must utilize the present wisely, guided by reason and justice. Exercise moderation even in your downtime.

This universe is either a cosmos organized by design or a jumble in chaos, yet it remains a universe. How can there be order within you if there is disorder in the whole? Especially when all is so scattered, spread out, and mutually responsive.

A dark disposition, an effeminate temperament, obstinacy, brutishness, immaturity, irrationality, deceit, vulgarity, fraudulence, despotism.

One is as much a stranger to the universe who is ignorant of its contents as one who is unaware of its workings. He who avoids the collective wisdom is akin to a deserter; he who closes the eyes of his understanding is blind; he who depends on others for what is essential in life is impoverished. One who separates himself from the universal reason due to discontent with life's events is like a festering sore on the world, for that same universal nature has brought forth both the events and you. He is a fragment torn from the community, severing his soul from the collective soul of rational beings.

Consider the philosopher without a cloak, another without books, and yet another who is nearly destitute saying, "I have no bread, yet I live by reason."—"My learning does not earn my livelihood, but I live by my reason."

Cherish the craft you have learned, no matter how modest, and be content with it. Live the rest of your days as one who has entrusted his entire being to the gods, conducting yourself neither as a tyrant nor as a slave to any person.

Reflect upon the era of Emperor Vespasian. You will observe the same patterns of life: individuals marrying, raising children, falling ill, passing away, engaging in conflict, celebrating, trading, farming, flattering others, displaying arrogance, harboring suspicion, conspiring, longing for the demise of others, complaining about their current circumstances, pursuing love, accumulating wealth, seeking political honors, and aspiring to royal status. Yet, the lives of those from Vespasian's time have ceased to exist. Consider also the era of Emperor Trajan; life was much the same, and it too has passed. Look further back across the ages and at entire civilizations to see how many, after significant struggles, quickly perished and decomposed back into the basic elements. More importantly, reflect on those you have personally witnessed who fixated on trivial pursuits, who failed to act in harmony with their true nature, who did not adhere to their principles nor find satisfaction in them. Remember to weigh the importance of your focus and efforts appropriately, for by doing so, you will avoid discontent when you engage in minor matters only to the extent that is necessary.

The names that once resonated with fame have now become archaic: Camillus, Caeso, Volesus, Leonnatus, followed by the likes of Scipio, Cato, Augustus, and in later times, Hadrian and Antoninus. All entities quickly fade into mere stories, and complete obscurity swiftly claims them. This holds true even for those whose deeds were once celebrated magnificently. As for the others, they vanish from memory as soon as their life's breath departs, no longer mentioned by anyone. And what value does perpetual memory hold? It is but a void. So, what should we dedicate our earnest efforts to? Only this: just thoughts, actions that contribute to the social good, words that are consistently truthful, and a mindset that welcomes whatever comes to pass as necessary, familiar, and emanating from a principle and source of the same nature.

Embrace your fate with open arms, as if you are entrusting yourself to Clotho, one of the Fates, to weave your destiny as she sees fit.

Remember, everything is ephemeral: both the one who remembers and what is remembered.

Always keep in mind that change is a constant in this world, and become comfortable with the idea that the universe's nature relishes in transforming what exists and in creating new entities akin to them. Everything that is, serves as a precursor to what will come into being. However, your thoughts are likely limited to seeds sown into the soil or a womb, which is a rather limited perspective.

Your life will end soon, and you have not yet attained simplicity, tranquility, or freedom from the fear of external harm, nor have you learned to universally offer kindness. You have not come to believe that wisdom lies solely in just action.

Study the guiding principles of people, even those considered wise, to understand what they shun and what they seek.

What you perceive as harmful does not reside in someone else's intent or in the changes and conditions of your body. So where does it lie? It lies within the part of you that has the capacity to judge what is evil. Therefore, if this judging part does not label anything as harmful, all is well. Even if the body suffers, burns, or decays, let the part that passes judgment remain steady, understanding that nothing is intrinsically good or bad if it can happen to both those who act against nature and those who act in accordance with it. Anything that affects both equally is neither natural nor unnatural.

Always think of the universe as a single living entity, with one substance and one soul. Notice how everything relates to the one vision of this single entity, how all things move together, and how everything co-operates in the creation of everything that exists. Consider the unbroken spinning of the thread and the intricate weaving of the web of existence.

You are a small soul carrying around a corpse, as Epictetus once said.

There is no misfortune in change, just as there is no benefit in simply existing because of change.

Time is akin to a river composed of successive events—a forceful current—because once something is seen, it is swept away only to be replaced by the next, which will also be swept away in turn.

Everything that occurs is as common and familiar as roses blooming in spring or fruit ripening in summer; this includes sickness, death, slander, betrayal, and any other events that delight or distress the unwise.

In the unfolding of events, what comes after is always appropriately aligned with what has gone before; this sequence is not just a random list with obligatory continuation, but it is a logical progression. Just as all elements of the universe are arranged in a harmonious whole, so too the emergence of new events is not just consecutive but exhibits a remarkable correlation.

Keep in mind Heraclitus' insight: that earth's demise is its transformation into water, water's demise is its transformation into air, air's demise is its transformation into fire, and the cycle reverses. Remember also those who lose sight of their destination, who dispute with the very logic that orchestrates the cosmos; the everyday occurrences that they should be familiar with strike them as odd. Realize that we should live and communicate with full awareness, not in a slumberous state, for even in sleep we appear to engage and converse. We should not, like children who mimic their parents, merely repeat and perform as we have been instructed without understanding.

If a divine being were to inform you that your life would end tomorrow or without a doubt the day after, you would likely feel indifferent about whether your death came on the second or the first day, unless you were excessively cowardly, for the difference is trivial. Likewise, consider it not significant to pass away after counting as many years as possible rather than tomorrow.

Reflect continuously on the multitude of physicians who have died after frequently furrowing their brows over their patients; the astrologers who, after confidently predicting others' demises; the philosophers who have pondered at length on death or immortality; the heroes who have perished after slaughtering countless foes; and the tyrants who have wielded their dominion over the lives of others with ruthless arrogance as though they were eternal; and consider the many cities that have been completely wiped out, like Helice, Pompeii, and Herculaneum, and countless more. Remember each person you have known, one after the other. One person lays another to rest, only to be interred by someone else in turn, and all within a brief span of time. In conclusion, always recognize how transient and insignificant human affairs are, and that what is today bodily fluid will tomorrow transform into a mummy or dust. Navigate through this brief existence in harmony with nature, and complete your life with satisfaction, just as a ripe olive might fall, grateful to nature for giving it life, and appreciative of the tree that bore it.

Be steadfast like a cliff where waves constantly crash; it remains unmoved and calms the raging waters around it.

Do not lament, "I am unfortunate because this has happened to me." Rather, declare, "I am fortunate that, although this has occurred, I remain untroubled, uncrushed by the present, unworried about the future." This event could happen to anyone, but not everyone would remain untroubled by it. Why regard this as a misfortune rather than that as good fortune? Do you define misfortune as anything that does not align with human nature, or as something against the intentions of human nature? But you are aware of what nature intends. Will this event prevent you from being just, generous, self-controlled, wise, and safe from rash judgments and deceit; from being modest, free, and possessing all other qualities that allow a person to fulfill their nature? Also, remember to apply this principle whenever you are annoyed: it is not a misfortune, but to bear it nobly is a sign of good fortune.

Reflecting on those who clung to life can be a rudimentary yet effective means to diminish the fear of death. What advantage have they gained over those who died early? Eventually, they too rest in their graves—Cadicianus, Fabius, Julianus, Lepidus, and the like, who saw many to their graves only to follow in the same path. The span between birth and death is brief, and consider the strife endured, the company kept, and the frailty of the body throughout this fleeting passage. Do not ascribe too much value to life when considering the vast expanse of time that stretches both behind and ahead of us, an endless void. In this eternal continuum, what is the difference between a life of three days and one of three generations?

Embrace the shortest path, the path of nature; thus, speak and act according to the most coherent reasoning. This approach liberates one from distress, conflict, pretense, and the need for show.

Workbook Exercises
Book IV

Self-Contained Existence

Marcus speaks of living an independent life, not requiring confirmation or affection from others. Reflect on areas in your life where you seek external validation. How can you cultivate more self-reliance?

Essence of Things

Marcus encourages us to consider the true essence of things beyond their appearances. Choose an object or situation and delve into its essence, examining your perceptions versus its reality.

Value of Rationality

Marcus places high value on living according to reason. Reflect on a recent decision and evaluate whether it was driven by reason or emotion. How did it affect the outcome?

Judgments and Opinions

Think about a recent judgment or opinion you had about someone else. How did this judgment serve you, and what would happen if you let it go?

Human Kindness

Reflect on the idea that kindness is mankind's natural state. When was the last time you acted with pure kindness, and what prompted it?

Meditations: Book V

W hen you wake with reluctance, remind yourself: I am rising for the tasks that befit a human. Why resent the very actions for which I exist and for which I was brought into the world? Am I destined merely to lie under the blankets and seek comfort? Is that truly more appealing? Were you created just for pleasure, not for effort and endeavor? Observe the small plants, the birds, the ants, the spiders, the bees, each contributing to their part in the grand scheme of nature. Can you, then, hesitate to fulfill your human duties and not rush to accomplish your natural purpose? Rest is indeed necessary, but even for rest, nature has set limits. These limits you surpass in indulgence of food and drink, taking more than needed, yet in your actions, you fall short of your potential.

You seem to care little for your own self, for if you did, you would cherish your nature and its intentions. Observe those passionate about their crafts; they tirelessly labor at their work, neglecting both wash and meal. Yet, you regard your own nature less than the carpenter does the craft of woodworking, the dancer the dance, the greedy their wealth, or the vain their fleeting fame. When such individuals are gripped by their passions, they forsake even food and sleep to hone their skills. Do you find the deeds that benefit society so contemptible, unworthy of your effort?

Consider, too, how simple it is to cast aside any troublesome or unsuitable thought, and to return swiftly to a state of calm.

Deem all words and actions aligned with nature as suitable for you, and don't be swayed by the criticism or speech of others. If an act or word is righteous, don't deem it beneath you. Others may follow their own principles and paths; pay them no mind. Instead, forge ahead, guided by your own character and the universal nature; their paths converge as one.

I will navigate the occurrences of life as nature dictates until I come to rest, surrendering my breath back to the air from which I draw it each day, returning to the soil that furnished the substance for my conception—my father's seed, my mother's blood, my nurse's milk. From this earth, I have drawn sustenance for years, the ground that supports my steps, even as I utilize it for countless needs.

Recognize that while some may not acknowledge your intellectual acuity, there are countless virtues that nature has indeed equipped you to display. Embrace and demonstrate the attributes wholly within your grasp: honesty, seriousness, tolerance for hard work, a distaste for excess, satisfaction with your lot and with simplicity, goodwill, candour, a rejection of needless things, and a disdain for pettiness. Behold the myriad traits you can immediately manifest, for which there is no excuse of natural deficiency or mismatch, and yet you may choose to fall short. Are you, by nature's design, destined to grumble, to hoard, to ingratiate yourself with insincerity, to criticize your own physical form, to court others' favor, to boast, to be incessantly unsettled in spirit? No, by the divine, you could have freed yourself from these burdens long ago. And if, perchance, you are accused of being naturally slow to comprehend, then endeavor to improve this too. Do not neglect it, nor find solace in your sluggishness.

When one person has helped another, he may be quick to regard this as a favor given, expecting gratitude or repayment. Another may not openly seek acknowledgment, yet internally, he considers the other person indebted to him, aware of his own actions. However, a third person may act benevolently without any thought of recognition, similar to how a vine simply produces grapes, seeking no reward once it has yielded its fruit. Just as a horse completes its run, a dog finds its prey, or a bee creates honey, so too should a person perform good deeds without a call for attention, moving on to the next task just as naturally as the vine bears fruit each season.

Should a person then act with such unobservant benevolence? Indeed, they should. Nevertheless, it is essential to be conscious of our actions: it is, after all, a fundamental aspect of a social creature to recognize its contributions to society, and to desire this recognition from its peers. What you say is true, but it's crucial to grasp the full implication of these words. Misinterpretation could lead one to the same misconceptions mentioned earlier, as even the most logical can be swayed by superficial reasoning. However, if you truly comprehend this principle, you need not worry that this awareness will hinder your ability to perform social duties.

An Athenian prayer: "Let it rain, let it rain, O mighty Zeus, upon the tilled fields of the Athenians and their vast plains." In truth, we should either not pray at all, or pray with such simplicity and grandeur.

We must interpret sayings like "Aesculapius has advised this person to take up horse-riding, to bathe in cold water, or to walk barefoot" with the same understanding as when it's said, "The nature of the universe has decreed illness, disfigurement, loss, or any such thing for someone." In the former, "prescribed" implies that Aesculapius has recommended this for the individual's health. In the latter, it signifies that whatever occurs to a person is appointed in harmony with their fate. This is our meaning when we say events are fitting for us, just as builders refer to stones as fitting well within a wall or pyramid when they are placed in proper alignment with one another.

For there is a universal fit and harmony. Just as the universe is composed of all physical bodies to form the entity that it is, so destiny is composed of all existing causes to be the force that it is. Even those who lack understanding grasp what I mean; they say, "Destiny has delivered this to that person." This, then, has been delivered and prescribed for them. We should welcome these events just as we would the treatments prescribed by Aesculapius. Many of his remedies are unpalatable, yet we accept them hoping for health. Consider the fulfillment and completion of what the universal nature deems good to be akin to your health. Therefore, embrace everything that occurs, even if it appears undesirable, because it contributes to the health of the universe and to the success and happiness of Zeus (the universe). For the universe would not have brought upon any individual what it has, if it were not beneficial for the whole. The nature of anything, whatever it may be, does not generate what is unsuitable to its guided purpose. There are two reasons, then, to be at peace with what befalls you: first, because it was carried out for you, appointed for you, and is in some way connected to you, having been determined by the oldest causes intertwined with your fate; and second, because every individual event is a source of joy and perfection to the universe's governing power, indeed, even to its survival. The wholeness of the cosmos is compromised if you sever any part from the synergy and sequence of its components or causes. And you do sever, to the extent of your influence, when you are discontent and attempt to reject any aspect of reality.

Do not be repelled, disheartened, or dissatisfied if you do not always act according to your highest principles. When you fall short, start again, and take comfort if most of your actions are in harmony with human nature. Embrace this return with affection; do not approach your philosophical practice as if it were a strict schoolmaster, but rather as one would apply a soothing remedy to painful eyes, like a sponge with egg whites, or as another might use a bandage or a cooling wash. By doing this, you will be sure to follow reason and find tranquility in it. Remember, philosophy demands only that which your nature truly needs; but you sometimes desire what is unnatural. You might ask, "Why, what is more delightful than what I am currently doing?" Yet, isn't this the very way that pleasure can mislead us? Reflect on whether virtues like greatness of spirit, freedom, simplicity, serenity, and devotion are not more delightful. For what can be more satisfying than wisdom itself, when you consider the assured peace and the smooth flow of all things that rely on the power of understanding and knowledge?

The nature of things is often cloaked in such complexity that it baffles many philosophers, not just the average thinkers but even the Stoics find it perplexing. Our agreements and beliefs are ever-shifting; no one is exempt from change. Reflect on the true nature of things: they are fleeting and of little value, and they might as well belong to the unvirtuous or the immoral as to anyone else. Consider the character of those around you; enduring even the most pleasant among them can be a struggle, to say nothing of tolerating oneself. In a world so filled with obscurity, muck, and incessant change—of matter, of time, of movement—what truly merits esteem or zealous pursuit is beyond me.

On the contrary, a man's duty is to find solace in himself, patiently awaiting the inevitable end without irritation at its delay. He should hold steadfast to two key tenets: first, that nothing will occur that is not in alignment with the universal nature; and second, that it is within his power to never act against his own divine spirit or inner guide, for no one else can force him to such action.

One should consistently question oneself: What purpose is my soul presently serving? In every situation, it is crucial to ask what part of me, which they refer to as the governing principle, is in operation? And whose spirit is it that I embody at this moment? Is it that of a child, a youth, a weak woman, a tyrant, a tame beast, or a wild animal?

The distinction between what is genuinely good and what is commonly deemed good by the masses can be discerned from a particular observation. If a person truly recognizes the inherent goodness of virtues like wisdom, self-control, justice, and courage, he would not tolerate any notion that contradicts these values after embracing them. Conversely, if an individual initially aligns with what the masses consider good—wealth, luxury, and fame—he is more likely to be amused by the witticisms of comedians regarding these pursuits.

Thus, even the general populace can sense the discrepancy. If the virtues were not inherently distinguished from common goods, the jest that one is so overwhelmed by their possessions that they lack even a private place for relief would not be met with disdain when applied to the former. It is only in reference to material excess that such a jest is considered fitting and clever. This begs the question: should we truly esteem and define as good those things which, once acquired in abundance, leave us as comically encumbered as the subject of the comedian's quip—that the possessor, amid his plenty, finds no room even to relieve himself?

I am a blend of the abstract and the physical; neither aspect will fade into nothingness, just as neither emerged from nothingness. Each part of me will transform through change into an element of the cosmos, and that will in turn morph into another element, continuing in an eternal cycle. Through this process of change, I exist, as did my ancestors, and this chain extends infinitely in both directions. This holds true irrespective of whether the cosmos operates in fixed cycles of change.

The faculty of reason and the practice of philosophy are self-sufficient; they originate from their own foundational principles and pursue their intended outcomes. This is why such deliberate actions are called 'right actions', a term that indicates they are moving along the correct path.

Things that are not essential to being human in its truest sense should not be considered possessions of a man. Such things are not demanded by our nature, nor does our essence guarantee them, nor do they contribute to the fulfillment of our natural purpose. Therefore, our ultimate goal does not reside in these externals, nor does our good lie in acquiring them. Furthermore, if these things were indeed integral to our being, it would be inappropriate for us to scorn or oppose them; praise would not be due to one who shows no desire for them, nor would one be considered virtuous for forgoing them if they were truly beneficial. However, it stands that the more a man can forgo these or similar things, or the more gracefully he can bear their loss, the greater his virtue and the more commendable he becomes.

Your prevailing thoughts shape the essence of your mind, as the soul takes on the color of your thoughts. So color it consistently with thoughts such as these: wherever a person can live, they can also live well. If one must live in a palace, then they can also live well in a palace. Furthermore, consider that each thing is created for a specific purpose, and it gravitates toward that purpose; its fulfillment and the good it can achieve lie in that direction. For a rational being, the highest good is found in community; as has been established, we are inherently social creatures. It is evident that lesser beings serve the greater, and among the living, those endowed with reason hold the highest rank.

Pursuing the unattainable is folly: it is inevitable that those who are ill-intentioned will act accordingly.

No event befalls a person that they are not naturally equipped to handle. Others experience the same events, and whether through ignorance or a display of resilience, they remain unaffected. It is regrettable, then, that naivety and vanity often outweigh wisdom.

External events do not touch the soul, nor do they gain entry or have the power to sway it; the soul is moved by its own impulses alone. Whatever assessments it chooses to make, it does so based on its perception of the events it encounters.

In one regard, human beings are most akin to me: I am bound to act benevolently towards them and tolerate them. Yet, when individuals obstruct my rightful actions, they become as indifferent to me as the sun, wind, or a wild animal. While these forces may hinder my actions, they cannot impede my intentions or inner state, which can adapt and transform any obstacle into an opportunity. Thus, what might obstruct my path can actually aid my progress and serve as assistance on my journey.

Honor that which is supreme in the universe; this essence utilizes and governs all. Similarly, honor the highest aspect within yourself, which is of the same nature. For it is this part of you that employs all else, and by this, your life is steered.

What does not injure the community cannot injure the individual. Whenever you perceive harm, remember this principle: if the community remains unscathed, so too am I. However, if the community is harmed, do not harbor resentment towards the offender. Instead, guide him to recognize his mistake.

Reflect often on the swift passage and vanishing of all things, both those that exist and those brought into being. Existence is akin to a river in ceaseless flow, and the endeavors of the world are in perpetual transformation, with causes leading to endless diversity; scarcely anything remains constant. Contemplate the vast expanse of time past and the future, this immeasurable gulf where all things are lost to oblivion. How then can one be wise to swell with pride or be troubled by these ephemeral matters, and allow oneself to be distressed? They are fleeting irritants, persisting but for a moment.

Consider the vast fabric of the universe, of which you are but a minuscule fragment; and of the grand expanse of time, in which you occupy merely a fleeting, undivided moment; and of fate, to which you are but a tiny contributor.

Should someone cause me harm? That is for them to consider. They possess their own character and actions. I possess what the nature of the cosmos has allotted to me; and I act according to what my own nature now dictates.

Let the governing part of your spirit remain unaffected by the sensations of the body, whether they be pleasures or pains; let it not merge with them, but instead delineate itself, confining these impulses to their bodily origins. However, when such sensations ascend to your consciousness due to the inherent empathy within a unified body, do not attempt to counter these feelings, for they are natural. Yet, let not the sovereign part of your being attach to this sensation any judgment of it being good or evil.

Live in harmony with the divine. A person lives with the gods by continually presenting them with a soul content with its lot and committed to its purpose, fulfilling the will of the spirit that Zeus has assigned as a guardian and guide to every individual—a fragment of himself, embodied in our capacity to understand and reason.

Would you become irate with someone for their body odors? What benefit is there in resentment? A person with a foul breath or pungent armpits cannot help the natural consequences of their body. Yet, it is argued, a person has the capacity for reason and can, through effort, discern and correct their faults. I commend you on such realization. Likewise, you have the power of reason: use your rationality to awaken theirs; enlighten them to their misstep, guide them. Should they heed your advice, you shall remedy the issue without resort to anger. There's no need for dramatics or indignation...

Live here as you would wish to live once you have departed; this is within your power. If others obstruct you, then leave life as one would leave a smoke-filled room, with no notion of being wronged. Why regard departure as troublesome? Until such an impetus arises, I stay, unfettered, with no one to prevent me from engaging in actions of my choosing; actions that align with the nature of a being endowed with reason and societal instincts.

The intelligence that permeates the universe is inherently communal. It has created the lesser for the sake of the greater, and has adapted the greater to interact harmoniously with one another. Observe how it has demarcated, coordinated, and allocated to each its rightful place, and how it has harmonized the finest of things into unity.

Reflect on your conduct towards the gods, your parents, siblings, children, mentors, those who cared for you in your early years, your friends, relatives, and your servants. Ask yourself if you have acted in such a way that it could be said of you:

Never has he wronged anyone in action or speech. Also, remember the multitude of experiences you have navigated, the challenges you have withstood: your life's narrative is now complete, your duty fulfilled. Consider the wonders you have witnessed, the myriad of delights and sorrows you have overlooked; the so-called honorable pursuits you have dismissed; and the generosity you have extended to those with ill intentions.

Why should the untrained and ignorant disturb one who possesses skill and knowledge? And which soul truly possesses skill and knowledge? It is the one that comprehends the beginning and the end, the one that understands the logic that imbues all matter and governs the cosmos with unchanging cycles.

Before long, you will be no more than dust or a skeletal frame, your name either remembered or lost to oblivion. Yet, a name is nothing but a sound, an echo. The acquisitions and accolades so dearly sought in life are hollow, decayed, and insignificant, comparable to puppies nipping at each other or children who argue, laugh, and then swiftly dissolve into tears.

Loyalty, modesty, justice, and truth have ascended to Olympus, leaving the vast earth behind. What, then, remains that holds you here? If sensory objects are ever-changing and unstable, if our senses are imprecise and easily deceived, and if the soul itself is merely a vapor emanating from blood. In such a transient world, renown is a hollow pursuit. Why not then await your end in peace, whether it leads to oblivion or a transformation? What is enough for this interim? Nothing more than to revere and give thanks to the deities, to do good unto others, to exercise forbearance and self-control; and to recall that anything beyond the scope of our fleeting flesh and breath is not ours to claim or control.

You can live in a steady state of contentment if you walk the correct path, if your thoughts and actions align rightly. This autonomy and commitment to justice are attributes shared by the divine spirit, the human soul, and every rational creature—none can be impeded by another. In these, find the fulfillment of your desires.

If what troubles you isn't born from your own misconduct, nor does it harm the collective good, why let it disturb you? What detriment does it bring to the common welfare?

Resist being swept away by mere appearances; instead, offer assistance to each based on their need and merit. And should they suffer losses in matters of little true importance, do not regard it as a real loss—for such a perspective is misguided. Just as an elder might request the return of a child's spinning top, recognizing it's just a toy, so too should you view these trivial matters.

When you stand before the crowd, voicing your concerns, have you forgotten what these things truly are? They may seem critical to others, but should you also be swayed by such trivialities? Once you considered yourself fortunate, yet that fortune was lost, inexplicably. But remember, true fortune isn't an external condition; it's the result of a well-ordered soul, virtuous feelings, and noble actions.

Workbook Exercises
Book V

Morning Reflections

Marcus speaks of waking up to do the work of a human being. Reflect on what you consider to be your work as a human being. How do you prepare yourself each morning to meet these responsibilities?

Overcoming Discomfort

Marcus reminds himself that to feel harmed by others' actions is to give them power over you. Think of a time when you felt wronged. How did you react, and how could a Stoic mindset have altered your response?

The Good Life

Reflect on Marcus' definition of a good life being one in harmony with nature. How do you align or struggle with this concept in your daily life?

Universal Change

Marcus accepts change as the universe's nature. Reflect on a change you are currently experiencing. How can you embrace it as part of the natural order of things?

Inner Circle

Reflect on the people you surround yourself with. How do they align with the values and virtues you hold dear? Are there adjustments to be made in your social circle that could better reflect your commitment to Stoic principles?

Meditations: Book VI

The essence of the cosmos is malleable and responsive, and the logic that steers it harbors no intent toward malice; it lacks the capacity for spite, and inflicts no suffering. All things evolve and reach fruition in accordance with this rational principle.

Your state of comfort or discomfort should not sway your commitment to your duties. Whether you are fatigued or well-rested, whether you face criticism or praise, or whether you are in the throes of death or engaged in another endeavor, it does not alter the necessity to perform the task at hand with diligence. Dying, after all, is just another process in life, and in this process, as in all others, excellence lies in executing what is before us to the best of our ability.

Turn your gaze inward. Do not overlook the inherent nature or worth of anything.

Everything in existence is transient, soon to transform. If all matter is one, then all will eventually dissipate into ether; if not, then all shall scatter into the void.

The guiding reason is conscious of its essence, its actions, and the substance upon which it exerts its influence.

The most noble form of retribution is to refrain from mirroring the misconduct of the one who has wronged you.

Find joy and solace in unity; transition seamlessly from one act of communal engagement to the next, keeping the divine in mind.

The sovereign element within us is self-activating, shaping both its own nature and its desires. It possesses the power to perceive and interpret all occurrences in a manner that aligns with its intentions.

Every event unfolds in harmony with the nature of the universe, as nothing occurs according to any external or separate nature—whether encompassing or encompassed by the universe, or even external and independent of it.

The cosmos is an entity of two possibilities: it is either a chaotic entanglement, a mingling and scattering of elements without order; or it is a coherent whole, characterized by order and guided by providence. If the former is true, then there is no reason to cling to a random assembly of matter and turmoil. In that case, why should I be concerned with anything other than my inevitable return to dust? And why should any agitation arise within me when the disintegration of my components is inevitable regardless of my actions? However, if the latter is the reality, then I hold in reverence, remain steadfast, and place my trust in the governing force of the universe.

When you find yourself unsettled by life's circumstances, make haste to regain your inner harmony. Do not linger in discord any longer than the situation necessitates; you will better maintain your composure by frequently recentering yourself.

Consider if you had both a step-mother and a mother: you would fulfill your duties to your step-mother, but it would be to your mother that you would constantly return. In this analogy, let the courtroom represent the step-mother and philosophy the mother. Frequently retreat into the arms of philosophy, for it is through her teachings that the trials faced in the courtroom seem bearable, and it is philosophy that makes you appear reasonable within it.

When faced with the allure of material pleasures, it helps to consider their true nature. The succulent dishes before us are merely the remains of once-living beings; the fine wine is but fermented grape juice; the luxurious purple garment, simply wool stained with the tint of a sea creature. These perceptions cut through the superficial and reveal the essence of things. This practice of seeing beyond the surface should apply to all aspects of life, especially when dealing with matters that demand our admiration and praise. We must peel away the layers of grandeur that language and society bestow upon them. Appearances have a potent ability to distort our judgment, often leading us astray precisely when we believe our endeavors to be most justified. Reflect on the insights of the philosopher Crates concerning Xenocrates, who himself is not exempt from such scrutiny.

The admiration of the multitude often rests on the simplest of objects: stones, timber, and trees such as figs, vines, and olives, admired for their cohesion and natural structure. A slightly more discerning group finds their admiration in living entities, like herds and flocks, valued for the life principle within them. Those with greater understanding appreciate entities endowed with a rational soul – not a universal one, but one distinguished by skill in a craft, expertise in a certain domain, or one that commands a number of servants.

But the truly enlightened individual esteems only the universal rational soul, one suited for civic life. Such a person's highest value lies in maintaining their own soul in a state of rationality and societal engagement. They commit to living according to reason and community, and seek fellowship with others who share these values. The enlightened soul thus rises above the material and transient, seeking fulfillment in the cultivation of the intellect and the betterment of communal life.

Certain things are rapidly coming into being, while others are just as quickly ceasing to be; and of those that are emerging, some are already fading away. The ceaseless flux and transformation are forever rejuvenating the world, much as the relentless progression of time perpetually renews the boundless span of ages. Within this ever-moving current, where nothing endures, what can truly be deemed valuable? It would be akin to becoming enamored with a sparrow in flight, only for it to vanish from view moments later. Such is the nature of human life—ephemeral, like the breath we exhale or the air we inhale and release continuously. In the same manner, the life force we breathe in at birth, just yesterday or the day prior, is destined to be surrendered back to the source from whence it came.

The processes of plants releasing moisture, the breathing of tamed and wild creatures, the perceptions formed by appearances, the pull of desires as if on puppet strings, the gathering in groups, or even the sustenance from food should not be held in high esteem; these are comparable to the body's discarding of unneeded sustenance. What then merits true appreciation? Surely not applause. Nor should we place worth on flattery, for such widespread acclaim is but superficial noise. If we were to dismiss the empty pursuit of fame, what of value is left? It is, in my view, to act and to exercise self-control in accordance with one's true nature, towards which all tasks and arts are directed. Every craft strives to shape its creation to fit its purpose; just as the gardener tends the vine, the horse trainer molds the steed, and the dog handler disciplines the canine, all aim for this harmony.

Education and the instruction of the young are endeavored with a clear purpose. The worth of teaching lies in this objective. If this is accomplished well, there should be no need to seek further. Would you not also learn to disvalue other things? Otherwise, you are not truly free, self-sufficient for your own contentment, nor without undue desire. For inevitably, you would harbor envy, jealousy, and distrust towards those who could deprive you of such things, and you would resent those in possession of what you prize. A person desiring these things is bound to live in turmoil; he will frequently blame the gods. However, holding your own intellect in high esteem will bring you peace within yourself, congruity with others, and accord with the divine, celebrating all that they provide and decree.

The workings of the natural world are all-encompassing, with the elements in constant motion above, below, and all around. Yet, the movement of virtue stands apart from these; it is of a more sacred nature and proceeds along its path with subtle grace, achieving its ends joyfully.

It's curious how people behave. They withhold praise from contemporaries, those with whom they share their time and space, yet they deeply value acclaim from future generations—those they have never met and never will. This preoccupation is akin to feeling upset that you weren't celebrated by those from past ages.

When you encounter a task that seems too challenging to tackle alone, do not deem it unachievable for humankind; and if any endeavor is within human capacity and aligns with human nature, believe that you, too, can accomplish it.

In athletic training, if someone accidentally scratches you or causes a head injury, we don't hold a grudge or become upset. Nor do we consider them deceitful. Still, we stay cautious around them, not as enemies or with suspicion, but we simply keep our distance. Apply this approach to life's other encounters. We should forgive many of the mistakes made by those around us, akin to opponents in a sports match. We have the choice to avoid conflict and bear no ill will or suspicion.

If someone can demonstrate to me that my thoughts or actions are incorrect, I am willing to change, for I am in pursuit of truth, which has never harmed anyone. It is the person who persists in his mistakes and ignorance who suffers harm.

I focus on fulfilling my own responsibilities; I am not troubled by other matters. They are either inanimate, irrational, or lost and unaware of the right path.

For the creatures devoid of reason, and indeed all objects and matters, use them thoughtfully and generously, as you possess reason and they do not. However, towards fellow humans, who are capable of reason, act with a sense of community and kindness. Always invoke the gods, and don't distress yourself with the duration of your endeavors; even a short time spent in such communion is valuable.

Alexander the Great and his stable boy were equalized by death; they were either integrated back into the fundamental elements of the universe or equally scattered into atoms.

Reflect on the multitude of events that occur simultaneously within us in a mere moment, affecting both body and soul. This will help you comprehend that in the vast continuum of the universe, which is a unified whole, countless events can—and do—occur at the same instant.

If someone were to ask you how to spell the name Antoninus, would you shout each letter with exertion? If they became irritable, would you respond in kind? Or would you calmly continue to spell out each letter? In the same way, in life, remember that every task is composed of elements. It is your responsibility to pay attention to these and, without becoming upset or angry at those who are irate with you, to calmly complete the task at hand.

It's unjust not to allow people to pursue what they believe is in line with their nature and beneficial. Yet, you essentially do the same when you become upset at their wrongdoing. They are driven by what they assume is good for them and in accordance with their nature. If this is not the case, then calmly teach and show them the right way without anger.

Death marks the end of sensory perceptions, the silencing of desires, the quieting of thoughts, and the end of serving the physical body.

It is disgraceful for the soul to succumb to the struggles of life before the body does.

Be vigilant not to become transformed into a ruler or to be tainted by such power; these transformations can occur. Therefore, maintain simplicity, goodness, purity, sincerity, authenticity, a love for justice, devotion to the divine, kindness, warmth, and dedication to all rightful deeds. Aim to embody the virtues that philosophy strives to instill. Honor the divine and assist humanity. Life is fleeting. The sole true yield of our earthly existence is a spirit of holiness and actions that foster community.

Emulate Antoninus as your guide. Recall his steadfast adherence to reason in his actions, his composure, his devout nature, his calm expression, his approachability, his indifference to superficial acclaim, and his commitment to understanding. Consider his meticulousness in scrutinizing and fully grasping matters before taking action; his forbearance towards those who unjustly faulted him, responding not with reproach but with understanding; his avoidance of haste; his disregard for slander; his scrupulousness in evaluating character and deeds; his avoidance of fault-finding, fear, suspicion, and sophistry.

Admire his contentment with minimal comforts—simple lodging, basic attire, plain food, few attendants. Observe his diligence and endurance, his ability to sustain long hours without need for physical relief, save at customary times. Reflect on his constancy and evenness in friendships, his willingness to entertain differing opinions, and his openness to being corrected. Note his devout yet non-superstitious piety.

Strive to imitate these qualities so that when your final moment arrives, your conscience may be as clear as his.

Reorient yourself to reality, grounding your perception in what is true. Recognize that the disturbances of your mind are like dreams, lacking substance when you awaken to clarity. Understand that you are composed of a body and a soul—the body, limited in its capacity to discern, is indifferent to the complexities around it, while the soul's concern lies only with what it can control, its own actions.

Acknowledge that only the present is within your grasp; past and future endeavors of the mind hold no sway over the now. Just as the natural functions of the body—like the work of the hands and feet—are not contrary to its nature, so too is a person's labor in alignment with their being when it fulfills human purpose. Therefore, if such labor is in accordance with one's nature, it cannot be a detriment. Live harmoniously within the bounds of your innate capabilities and the immediate moment, engaging with life's tasks as naturally as limbs perform their designated roles.

Reflect upon the fleeting nature of pleasures enjoyed by those who commit acts of robbery, patricide, or tyranny. These acts, though possibly bringing momentary joy, are fundamentally at odds with the principles of a just and virtuous life.

Consider how artisans, skilled in their respective crafts, may adjust their work to some extent to accommodate the layman's understanding. Yet, they remain steadfast to the core principles of their art, never fully abandoning the guidelines that ensure their work's integrity. Isn't it remarkable that an architect or a doctor should honor the tenets of their professions more than a man honors the principles of reason? This reason is not only intrinsic to humanity but also shared with the divine.

Asia and Europe are mere segments of the cosmos, every ocean merely a droplet within it; Mount Athos is but a speck. Our current moment is just an instant in infinity. Everything is small, mutable, and fleeting. All arise from the same universal creative force, whether directly or as a consequence. Thus, the gaping mouth of a lion, venom, and all that causes harm, such as thorns or mud, are secondary creations of the majestic and the beautiful. Do not regard them as separate from that which you hold in reverence. Instead, cultivate a correct understanding of the origin of all things.

One who has witnessed the events of the present has seen all that has occurred since the beginning of time and all that will ever happen in the unending future; for all phenomena are related by nature and are similar in their essence.

Regularly reflect on the interconnectedness of all things in the cosmos and their inter-dependence. In a sense, all elements are intertwined and, as such, there is a kinship among them; for each element follows another, aligned through active interaction, a harmonious collaboration, and the oneness of all matter.

Embrace the circumstances you've been given and the community among whom you've found your place. Love them genuinely and wholeheartedly.

An instrument or a vessel performs its function effectively even without the presence of its creator, and thus is deemed successful. Yet, within the creations of nature, there exists the enduring essence of the force that shaped them. Therefore, it is more appropriate to honor this force, and to understand that living and acting in alignment with its purpose means that all within you resonates with reason. Similarly, within the universe, everything that is part of it operates in harmony with reason.

If you consider things beyond your control to be good or bad for you, then inevitably, when you encounter misfortune or lose a perceived good, you will find fault with the gods and harbor resentment towards people who you believe caused or could cause such events. This attitude often leads to unfairness, as we incorrectly assign importance to these external factors. However, if we recognize that only the things within our control can truly be considered good or bad, then we have no grounds to blame the gods or to be antagonistic towards others.

We are all contributors to a shared purpose, some with conscious intention and others unwittingly, reminiscent of Heraclitus' description of sleeping people unknowingly participating in the world's events. People engage in this collective endeavor in various ways, including those who criticize or resist the course of events. The universe requires even these dissenting roles. The important consideration for you is to discern what type of contributor you choose to be. For the sovereign force that orchestrates the cosmos will surely utilize you appropriately, integrating you among the diverse agents whose efforts serve a unified objective. Aim not to be like the trivial and laughable character in a play, as referenced by the philosopher Chrysippus.

The sun does not attempt the rain's task, nor does Aesculapius take up the role of the earth to bear fruit. Just as each star in the heavens is distinct, yet all contribute to a common goal.

If the divine powers have preordained my fate and all that must befall me, they have surely done so with wisdom. It is difficult to conceive of a god without the capacity for foresight. And what reason would they have to do me harm? What benefit would it bring to them or to the cosmos, which is under their care? If they haven't decreed my individual destiny, then at least they have ordained the grand scheme of things. The events that naturally follow within this framework should be welcomed and embraced by me. But to think the gods decide nothing at all is a profane notion; and if one were to believe such a thing, it would nullify the need for sacrifices, prayers, oaths, and all acts we perform under the impression of their watchful presence. However, if the gods do not concern themselves with our affairs, then the responsibility falls upon me to govern myself and to seek out what is truly beneficial.

That which aligns with one's own nature and essence is beneficial. For me, as Antoninus, my city is Rome; as a human being, it is the world. Thus, what benefits these communities is what benefits me. Everything that occurs to any individual aligns with the interests of the universe, and that alone could suffice. But beyond this, you will notice a universal principle: what is advantageous for one person often benefits others as well. Here, 'advantageous' refers to things that are neutral, neither inherently good nor evil.

Just as the repeated viewing of the same events in an amphitheater grows tedious due to the lack of variety, so too can life become monotonous; for all things, whether celestial or terrestrial, are fundamentally the same and from the same source. How long, then, can this go on?

Remember always that a multitude of people from every profession, nation, and era have passed away — your thoughts should even include figures such as Philistion, Phoebus, and Origanion. Now, shift your focus to other individuals. We are destined to join those who have already passed: numerous eloquent speakers, esteemed philosophers like Heraclitus, Pythagoras, and Socrates, valiant warriors of ancient times, successive generals and rulers. Also among them are the likes of Eudoxus, Hipparchus, Archimedes — individuals of sharp intellect, vast understanding, dedicated to their work, adaptable, and who viewed the fleeting and transient human life with a certain irreverence, like Menippus and others of his ilk. Reflect that all these individuals have long since turned to dust. What detriment has this caused them; and what of those whose names are entirely forgotten? There is one thing of great importance: to live a life of truth and fairness, with kindness, even towards those who are deceitful and unjust.

When you seek joy, consider the virtues of those around you. Reflect on the energy of one, the humility of another, the generosity of a third, and other admirable traits of yet others. There is great delight in witnessing virtues manifested in the behavior of those we interact with, especially when such examples are plentiful and readily observed. Thus, we should always keep them in our sight.

Just as you do not lament having a certain body weight rather than being three hundred pounds, do not lament living a certain number of years rather than more. Just as you are content with the body that has been given to you, be content with the lifespan allotted to you.

Try to convince others with reason, but if justice demands, act even if it's against their will. Should someone forcefully oppose you, turn to contentment and tranquility, using the obstacle to practice another virtue. Remember, your action was conditional; you did not aim for the impossible. What did you seek? Simply to make an effort. And you succeed if you accomplish the intended actions.

One who values fame sees another's success as their own gain; one who cherishes pleasure sees their own feelings as their primary good; but one with understanding sees their own actions as their own true good.

We have the ability to withhold judgment on matters, thus keeping our soul undisturbed; for it is not events themselves that trouble us, but our opinions about these events.

Train yourself to listen intently to others, striving to truly understand their perspective.

What harms the collective, harms the individual as well.

If sailors insulted the captain or patients the doctor, could they heed any advice? How could the captain or doctor ensure the safety and health of those under their care?

Countless people who entered this world with me have already departed.

Honey seems bitter to those with jaundice, water frightens those with rabies, and children cherish a ball. Why should anger arise in me? Is a misconception not as influential as the jaundice's bile or the rabid dog's venom?

No one can prevent you from living by your own rational nature; nothing will occur that is against the universal nature's logic.

Consider the types of people who seek others' approval, the motives behind it, and the methods they use. Remember how quickly time conceals all things and how much it has already concealed.

Workbook Exercises
Book VI

Inner Freedom

Marcus discusses the concept of inner freedom, regardless of external circumstances. Reflect on a situation where external factors greatly affected you. How can you cultivate a sense of inner freedom despite these factors?

Self-Examination

Consider the idea of examining your own thoughts as if they were someone else's. Reflect on the thoughts you've had today. Are they rational and aligned with your values, or do they require some adjustment?

Responding to Mistreatment

Marcus advises kindness in response to mistreatment. Recall a time when you were treated unfairly. How did you respond, and how does Marcus' advice challenge you to respond differently in the future?

The Role of Opinion

Reflect on Marcus' belief that opinions do not reflect reality but our own thoughts. How do your opinions shape your reality, and are there any you need to let go of for your well-being?

Distractions and Purpose

Reflect on what distracts you from living a life of purpose. What strategies can you employ to minimize these distractions and focus on what truly matters?

Meditations: Book VII

E vil is a recurring phenomenon, a theme as old as time, witnessed over and over. With each event that unfolds, remind yourself that it is a repeat of what has been. The same patterns fill ancient texts, the sagas of the middle ages, and the tales of our era. They saturate our cities and homes. There is nothing truly new under the sun—everything is both commonplace and fleeting.

How can our beliefs wither unless the thoughts that nourish them are snuffed out? You possess the power to kindle those thoughts at will. I am capable of holding the perspective I should on any subject. If that is within my control, why should I be perturbed? External circumstances have no intrinsic connection to my mind. Embrace this mindset, and you shall remain steadfast. To reclaim your life is within your grasp. Observe the world as you once did; therein lies the revival of your being.

The trivial pursuits of life—stage plays, livestock, martial drills, simple playthings for animals, the diligent toil of ants, the scurrying of mice, marionettes guided by strings—are all part of the same tableau of existence. Amidst these distractions, it is your responsibility to maintain a good-natured demeanor, not one of arrogance, while recognizing that a person's value is equivalent to what they concern themselves with.

In conversation, focus on the substance of what's being discussed. In action, be attentive to the proceedings. In listening, discern the ultimate purpose at once; in observing, scrutinize what each action symbolizes. It is in this dual awareness of purpose and symbolism that one navigates through the superficial to grasp the substantive essence of life's engagements.

Your understanding is a tool provided by universal nature, meant to be applied to tasks for which it is suited. If your understanding is adequate, employ it diligently. If not, step aside for someone more capable, unless there is a compelling reason to persevere. Alternatively, do the best you can, seeking assistance from someone who can complement your efforts towards the common good. What matters is the utility and the benefit to society, whether achieved alone or with others.

The fleeting nature of fame should not distract you; many who were once celebrated are now forgotten, and many who have celebrated others have passed away.

Accepting help is not a sign of weakness but a strategic approach to fulfilling your role. Like a soldier who must scale the walls in a siege, if you cannot do it alone due to a limitation, it is sensible to accept assistance. The objective is to overcome the obstacle, not necessarily to do it unaided.

Do not let the prospect of future events cause you anxiety. When the time comes to face them, you will be equipped with the same reason and logic that guide you in the present.

The interconnectedness of all things is profound and sacred, with hardly anything standing alone. All components of the universe are interwoven, creating an orchestrated whole. There is but one cosmos consisting of all things, one divine presence that exists throughout, one underlying matter, one law governing all, and a singular, shared reason within all sentient beings, leading to a unified truth. This suggests that there is also one ideal form of existence for all creatures that share this common rationality.

Material entities quickly dissolve into the greater whole of the universe, while the causal nature of things is swiftly integrated back into the collective reason. Similarly, the memory of all things is rapidly erased by the passage of time.

The rational being is naturally aligned with reason in its actions.

Stand upright on your own, or be set right by others. As the limbs of a single body work in unison, so too should rational beings, though distinct, collaborate towards a common purpose. This understanding becomes clearer when one regularly contemplates being an integral part of the collective of rational beings. If you merely consider yourself a segment (meros) rather than a member (melos), you have not yet learned to love your fellow beings genuinely. Your acts of kindness are performed out of obligation, not from the joy of benefiting others or recognizing it as benefiting yourself.

Let whatever happens impact the parts of you that are susceptible to such events. Those parts can react if they choose. But I am not harmed unless I regard the occurrence as harmful, which is a perception within my control.

Like the unwavering quality of gold, emerald, or purple dye, I too must remain good, no matter the actions or words of others. The emerald must maintain its color, and I must maintain my virtue.

The mind does not trouble itself—it does not become frightened or pained from within. If another can cause it fear or pain, let them try. The mind, through its own judgement, will not create turmoil for itself. Let the body, if it is able, ensure it suffers no harm and speak out if it does. The soul, the part that can experience fear or pain, which holds complete control over its own opinions, will endure no suffering, for it will not adopt a judgement that leads to such suffering. The guiding principle within desires nothing except what it decides it needs; thus, it remains untroubled and unobstructed, as long as it does not disturb or impede itself.

Happiness is a benevolent spirit. And to you, O imagination that arises unbidden, I say depart as you came, by the gods, I beseech you. I have no need of you. You arrive as is your custom, but I hold no anger towards you: simply go away.

Change is an essential and inevitable part of life and the universe. Just as wood must be altered to create a fire for a bath, and food must be transformed to nourish the body, change is a constant process that enables usefulness and progress. It is a natural and necessary force within the universal nature.

All things are part of the universal substance and are swept along like bodies in a powerful stream, working together with the whole, just as the parts of our body work in harmony with each other. Time has consumed great minds like Chrysippus, Socrates, and Epictetus, and this will hold true for all people and things.

The only concern should be to avoid acting against the natural constitution of humanity, either in manner, timing, or action that is not permitted. This alignment with nature and the proper functioning of one's role within it is paramount.

The time when you will forget all things is approaching, and the time when all will forget you is equally near.

It is innate in humans to love even those who err. This feeling arises when you recognize that the person erring is a relative, acting not out of malice but out of ignorance and without intent, and that mortality looms over both of you; most importantly, that their actions have caused you no real harm, for they have not impaired your ability to reason.

Just as nature crafts from a single substance, shaping a horse out of what seems like wax, then breaking it down to form a tree, then a human, and so on, each form exists but briefly. The process of breaking down is no more grievous than the process of creation.

A constant frown is profoundly against our nature; habitual frowning eventually erases beauty, until it cannot be restored. From this, deduce that such behavior is illogical. If we lose even the awareness of our misdeeds, what purpose is there left in life?

Nature, the sovereign of all, will swiftly transform everything you see and from their essence forge new things, which in turn will be reshaped, ensuring the world remains perpetually fresh.

When someone wrongs you, reflect at once on what beliefs about good and evil led to their actions. Understanding this, you will feel compassion rather than surprise or anger. For you either share the same view of good as they do or hold a similar one. Therefore, it's your responsibility to forgive. If you do not consider such things good or evil, then you'll find it easier to empathize with one who is mistaken.

Focus less on what you lack and more on what you possess. Of your assets, choose the finest and consider how ardently you would desire them if you did not have them. Yet, be cautious that your satisfaction does not lead you to overestimate their worth, to the point where their loss would disturb you.

Turn inward. The mind governed by reason is self-sufficient, finding contentment in justice and thus achieving peace.

Dismiss fanciful thoughts. Halt the impulses that tug at your will. Focus on the present. Comprehend fully what transpires, be it related to you or others. Analyze and categorize each event by its cause and its substance. Contemplate your mortality. Let any wrongdoing committed remain where it occurred.

Pay close attention to the words spoken. Engage your mind with the actions taking place and the agents behind them.

Embellish your character with straightforwardness and humility, and remain indifferent to matters that neither define nor detract from virtue. Embrace humanity. Emulate the divine. As the poet proclaims, Law governs all—and this is sufficient to recall that Law is supreme.

On death: Whether it be a scattering, a transformation back into elements, or total cessation, it is simply either non-existence or alteration.

Regarding pain: Pain that cannot be endured ultimately takes us away, yet pain that persists can be endured; the mind can keep its peace by turning inwards, and its governing principle remains unharmed. As for the parts of us that suffer from pain, let them judge if they are able.

Concerning fame: Reflect on the inner nature of those who desire fame, what their minds are like, what they shun, and what they strive for. Realize that just as successive layers of sand bury the ones beneath, so too are past deeds quickly obscured by those that follow in life.

From Plato: Consider a person with a noble spirit who contemplates all of time and the whole of reality. Do you think he would deem human life to be of significant importance? He would not—Plato asserts. Such a person would also regard death as nothing detrimental—of course not.

From Antisthenes: There is a kingly honor in acting kindly while enduring criticism. It is a lowly thing when our facial expression is under control, conforming to our will, but our mind remains unruly and unsettled within us.

It's pointless to get upset over things, as they are indifferent to our distress.

Let us bring pleasure to the immortal gods and ourselves.

Life should be harvested like ripe grain: one person comes into existence, another passes away.

If the gods seem indifferent to me and my offspring, there must be a reason for it.

For I possess what is good and just within me.

We should not join in others' lamentations or give in to excessive grief.

From Plato: To the argument presented, I would offer a sound rebuttal: You are mistaken if you believe that a truly worthy person ought to weigh the risks of life and death. Instead, he should be solely concerned with whether his actions are just or unjust, the deeds of a virtuous or a wicked person.

Indeed, citizens of Athens, the truth is this: wherever a person has decided the best place for him to be, or has been positioned by a leader, there he ought to remain and face the risks, disregarding all else, be it death or any other fear, rather than face the disgrace of abandoning his post.

However, my esteemed peer, contemplate whether what is honorable and virtuous is not distinct from mere survival. For a person who is truly a man, the length of his life is a matter to be set aside. One must not cling to life. These concerns should be entrusted to the divine, adopting the belief, as women often say, that no one can evade his fate. The subsequent question should be how he may best spend the time he is allotted to live.

Gaze upon the movements of the stars as if you were journeying alongside them; and often reflect on the transformation of elements into one another. Such meditations cleanse the sullied thoughts of earthly existence.

This insight from Plato suggests that when one speaks of human affairs, they should observe earthly activities as though from a higher vantage point. Look upon gatherings, military camps, farm work, weddings, agreements, births, passings, the hubbub of legal proceedings, secluded places, diverse cultures, celebrations, mournings, and marketplaces – a mix of everything and a harmonious arrangement of opposites.

Reflect on historical epochs; observe the vast shifts in governance. Anticipate the future too, for it will likely mirror the present, bound by the same patterns. Thus, to have observed life for four decades is akin to observing it for millennia. What more can be revealed to you?

That which originates from the soil returns to it,
But what is born of celestial essence
Ascends back to celestial spheres. This signifies either the separation of intertwined atoms or a kindred scattering of lifeless particles.

Despite our efforts with sustenance, drinks, and clever tricks
To divert the path of fate and elude demise,
The wind sent by the gods
We must bear, and labor on without grievance.

Someone else may excel in overcoming an adversary, but that does not make them more community-minded, more humble, better prepared to handle life's events, or more forgiving of others' mistakes.

In any endeavor that aligns with the reason shared by gods and humans, we have no cause for fear: when we can gain benefit from actions that are effective and in harmony with our true nature, we can trust that they bring no harm.

At all times and in every place, it is within your capacity to peacefully accept your current situation, to act with fairness toward those around you, and to apply your reasoning diligently to your thoughts, ensuring that they are thoroughly scrutinized before you accept them.

Avoid becoming preoccupied with the guiding principles of others; instead, focus directly on the path that nature has laid out for you. This includes both the universal nature that directs the events in your life, and your individual nature that dictates your actions. Each being should act in accordance with its own design; and just as all things are created with rational beings in mind, with the lesser serving the greater among non-rational beings, rational beings are meant to interact with one another.

The foremost principle in human nature is to be social. The second is to resist being swayed by the body's demands, for it is the unique role of rational and conscious thought to set its own boundaries, and not be overwhelmed by the impulses of the senses or desires, which are animalistic in nature. Rational thought must maintain its dominance, not allowing itself to be overruled by these lower impulses, for it is designed by nature to govern them. The third aspect of our rational nature is to avoid falsehood and self-deception. Therefore, let the mind adhere steadfastly to these principles and proceed with confidence, for then it will possess what truly belongs to it.

Consider yourself as having already lived your life up to this point, and having reached a sort of death. From now on, live in accordance with nature for the time you have remaining.

Embrace only what occurs in your life, woven into the fabric of your destiny. For what could be more fitting for you?

In the face of life's events, remember those who have experienced similar circumstances, how they became upset, regarded these events as oddities, complained about them, and are now gone—vanished. Why then do you choose to react in the same manner? Why not leave these needless troubles to those who instigate them and those who are disturbed by them? Why not focus entirely on the proper use of the events that occur to you? By doing so, you will handle them well, and they will become resources for your endeavors. Pay attention to yourself and commit to being a virtuous person in every action you take. And bear in mind...

Turn your gaze inward; the source of goodness resides within, and will continuously flow if you persistently excavate it.

The body should be well-knit and display no awkwardness in movement or posture. Just as the mind is reflected in the face through an expression of intelligence and decency, so too should the body exhibit these qualities. However, this should be achieved naturally, without pretense.

The craft of living rightly is akin to the art of wrestling rather than dancing, in that it must be prepared to deal with sudden and unforeseen challenges with resilience and steadiness.

Pay close attention to those whose approval you seek and understand their guiding principles. By doing so, you will neither find fault with those who err unintentionally, nor will you crave their approval once you recognize the origins of their judgments and desires.

A philosopher declares that every soul is unwittingly stripped of truth; and in the same vein, it is stripped of justice, self-control, kindness, and the like. It is essential to remember this continually, for it will make you more compassionate towards everyone.

In the face of pain, remind yourself that it carries no shame and does not degrade your rational or social intelligence. Pain does not harm your ability to think or interact socially. Remember what Epicurus said: pain is neither endless nor unbearable if you recognize its limits and don't exaggerate it in your mind. Also, consider that many discomforts, like extreme sleepiness, being overheated, or loss of appetite, are akin to pain without us categorizing them as such. So when you find yourself unsettled by any of these, remind yourself that you are simply experiencing a form of pain.

Be cautious not to adopt the attitudes of those who lack humanity towards others.

How can we be sure that Telauges was not of a nobler character than Socrates? It's not sufficient to say that Socrates faced a more dignified death, debated more effectively with sophists, endured cold nights with greater resilience, or nobly refused to arrest Leon of Salamis. Nor should we focus on claims of his ostentatious behavior in public—such accounts are dubious. Instead, we should consider the essence of Socrates' character: whether he maintained a just and pious disposition, neither perturbed by the wickedness of others nor submissive to anyone's ignorance, nor bewildered by his share of universal events, nor seeing it as unbearable, nor allowing his rational mind to be affected by the sufferings of the body.

Nature has intertwined the mind and the body, yet it has also provided you the capacity to limit your concerns to your own realm of control; it is entirely feasible to live with the virtue of the divine, unnoticed by others. Remember this always, and also remember that it takes remarkably little to lead a contented life. Even if you have given up on becoming an expert in debate or a master of natural philosophy, do not lose hope of achieving freedom, modesty, sociability, and piety.

You have the ability to live free from coercion and with a serene mind, regardless of the clamor of the world or the physical challenges to your body. Nothing prevents your mind from remaining calm, from making fair assessments of the world, and from engaging effectively with whatever it encounters. Let your judgement recognize the true nature of things, regardless of common misconceptions, and let your actions embrace what comes your way as an opportunity for virtue. Whether it pertains to human society or higher divine reasoning, each event is neither unprecedented nor overwhelming but is familiar and fitting material for your faculties to work upon.

Moral excellence is found in living each day as if it were your last, without succumbing to overexcitement, lethargy, or deceit.

Consider the gods: eternal and untroubled despite enduring humanity's flaws, continuously caring for them. You, whose time is finite, why feel burdened by others' wrongdoings, especially when you share in human imperfections? It's absurd to attempt escaping the vices of others when you should instead escape your own, which is within your power.

What is not aligned with reason and society, your rational and communal nature rightly deems lesser.

When you perform a good deed and it's accepted, don't seek a third reward, such as recognition or repayment. This is the folly of those who don't understand the value of virtue itself.

We never tire of receiving what benefits us. And since acting in accord with nature is beneficial, one should never tire of benefiting others in this way.

The divine force set the universe in motion. Now, everything occurs in a sequence of cause and effect, or the universe's guiding principle leads without rational design. Keeping this in view will aid in maintaining tranquility amidst life's events.

Workbook Exercises
Book VII

The Nature of Evil

Marcus suggests that evil is a form of ignorance. Think of a time when you witnessed or experienced what you perceived as evil. How does reframing it as ignorance change your understanding of the situation?

Dealing with Others' Opinions

Reflect on the impact others' opinions have on you. How can you detach from these to live more in line with your own values and judgments?

Life as a Play

Marcus compares life to a play. Reflect on the role you are currently playing. Are you content with it, and how authentically are you embracing this role?

Meditations: Book VIII

T his contemplation helps to dispel the craving for superficial accolades: it is beyond your capability to have led your entire life, or at least from your youth, as a philosopher. This truth is evident not only to others but to yourself; you have strayed from a disciplined path. Thus, the acclaim of living as a philosopher is unattainable, and your way of life is at odds with such a title.

If you recognize the essence of the matter, cast aside concerns of perception by others. Find satisfaction in living the remainder of your days in harmony with your intrinsic nature. Focus on this, and don't get sidetracked. You have roamed enough, searching for contentment in logic, riches, fame, pleasure, and found it in none. Where, then, does happiness lie? In fulfilling the duties that human nature demands.

And how can one fulfill these duties? By adhering to fundamental principles that guide emotions and actions. Which principles? Those concerning what is genuinely good or bad: the conviction that nothing is truly good for a person unless it fosters justice, moderation, courage, and freedom; and nothing is truly bad except what leads to the opposite of these virtues.

When you undertake any action, question its impact on yourself. Will you regret it? You are mortal, and soon everything will end. If what you are doing is the work of a rational and social being, adhering to the same divine laws, what more do you require?

Consider the lives of great leaders like Alexander, Gaius, and Pompeius versus philosophers like Diogenes, Heraclitus, and Socrates. The philosophers understood the nature of things, their causes, and their essence, living by principles that aligned with reason. The leaders, however, were burdened with countless obligations and enslaved by their desires.

Acknowledge that regardless of your distress, people will continue their behaviors. The most important thing is not to let yourself be disturbed; everything happens according to the universe's nature. Soon, you will be as forgotten as Hadrian and Augustus.

Focus on your responsibilities with clarity. Remember your duty to be virtuous, fulfilling what human nature requires. Act according to what seems most right to you, but do so kindly, humbly, and sincerely.

The essence of the cosmos is in a constant state of flux, transferring elements from one state to another, transforming and relocating them. This cycle of change is natural, and nothing genuinely novel arises that should incite fear. All experiences are recognized, though their arrangement may shift.

A nature that functions optimally is at peace with itself; a rational being achieves this by affirming only what is true and within its grasp, engaging in societal contributions, and by restraining desires and aversions to what it can control. It finds fulfillment in what the universal nature allocates, of which every individual nature is a part, just as leaves are to a tree. However, unlike the leaves, human nature is part of a conscious, unobstructed whole that is intelligent and just, distributing resources and opportunities impartially and according to merit.

When evaluating, it's not about comparing individual aspects in isolation but considering the entirety of one entity against the entirety of another.

If you lack the time or means to engage in extensive study, you can still exercise control over your ego, rise above pleasure and pain, be indifferent to fame, and show patience and care towards the ignorant and unthankful.

Resolve to no longer be heard criticizing life at court or your own circumstances.

Repentance serves as a form of self-criticism for having overlooked something beneficial; what is truly good must be beneficial, and the virtuous individual should pursue such things. However, a genuinely virtuous person would never regret turning away from sensual pleasures. Therefore, pleasure is neither inherently good nor beneficial.

Consider any object: what is it in its essence? What are its material and form? What purpose does it serve in the world, and for how long does it endure?

When you wake up feeling unwilling, remind yourself that engaging in societal activities aligns with your nature and that of humanity, whereas the act of sleeping is shared with beings incapable of reason. What is natural to an individual is uniquely theirs, more fitting to their nature, and usually more satisfying.

Always, and whenever possible, apply the principles of natural science, ethics, and logic to each thought that affects your mind.

Upon meeting another person, immediately consider their views on what is good or evil. If their beliefs about pleasure, pain, honor, disgrace, death, and life are known to you, then their actions will not seem unexpected, and you'll understand they are driven by their beliefs.

Remember, it's as illogical to be shocked by the world's happenings as it is to be surprised by a fig tree bearing figs; similarly, a doctor or a sailor should not be taken aback by sickness or adverse winds.

Keep in mind that adapting your views when corrected is as much a part of freedom as is sticking to your errors. Your actions are yours alone, arising from your decisions and thoughts, and from your own intellect.

If you have the power to act, then why delay? If it is beyond your control, who are you to blame? Atoms or gods? Such blame is senseless. One should not assign fault. If possible, address the cause; if not, strive to amend the situation itself; and if that too is impossible, why bother complaining? Actions should always be driven by purpose.

What has passed away does not vanish from the cosmos. It remains and transforms within this realm, decomposing into its elemental parts, which belong both to the universe and to you. And these elements, too, undergo change without complaint.

Every being serves a purpose, as does a horse or a grapevine. Should this surprise you? Even the sun would declare its utility, and the other deities would concur. Then, for what purpose do you exist? For mere pleasure? Consider whether this aligns with reason.

In all things, nature is as concerned with their end as with their beginning and persistence, similar to a person tossing a ball. What benefit does the ball gain from its ascent, or what loss from its descent or even its fall? The same holds for a bubble, whether intact or burst, or a candle, whether lit or extinguished.

Consider the body, turned inside out, and see its true nature; observe it when aged, what it becomes, and its appearance when ill.

Both those who give praise and those who are praised are fleeting, as are those who remember and those who are remembered. All of this occurs within a small corner of the world, and even here there is no consensus, not even within an individual. Moreover, the entire globe is but a speck.

Focus on what lies directly in front of you, be it a thought, an action, or a word.

You endure hardship justly: for you always postpone being virtuous today in favor of tomorrow.

When I take action, I do it for the benefit of humankind. When something happens to me, I accept it and attribute it to the gods and the universal origin from which all events unfold.

Consider the repugnance of bathing - oil, sweat, grime, dirty water, all sorts of unpleasantries - such is life in all its parts.

Lucilla witnessed Verus's death and then she died. Secunda saw Maximus pass away, then Secunda died. Epitynchanus watched Diotimus die, and then he too passed. Antoninus observed Faustina's death, then he departed. This pattern holds for all. Celer saw Hadrian die, and then Celer met his end. What of the keen-minded individuals, those regarded as seers or those who were swollen with pride? Where are they now? Consider individuals like Charax, Demetrius the Platonist, Eudaemon, and others of their ilk. All of them are long gone, some scarcely remembered, others relegated to the realm of legend, and some even faded from the tales themselves. Remember this: your own being, this small composite, must eventually disintegrate, or your feeble life force will be extinguished or taken and transplanted elsewhere.

A man finds contentment in performing the duties inherent to his nature. For a man, these include showing kindness to his fellow humans, rejecting the impulses of the senses, judging outward appearances with fairness, and understanding the nature of the cosmos and the events within it.

There are three kinds of relationships a person has: one with the physical body that one inhabits; another with the divine origin that is the source of all things for everyone; and a third with the people one coexists with.

Pain is only detrimental to the body or the soul. If to the body, let the body assess it. If to the soul, the soul has the power to keep its peace and not deem pain as a malevolence. Every assessment, impulse, longing, and aversion is internal; no harm can truly permeate to such heights.

To control one's imaginings, remind yourself often: now it is within my control to ensure this soul harbors no wickedness, desire, or disturbance; when observing all things, I understand their essence and engage with each according to its worth. Recall this ability you possess by nature.

Speak in the senate and to every individual, no matter who, with due propriety, without pretense: employ straightforward language.

Reflect upon the court of Augustus: his wife, daughter, descendants, forebears, sister, Agrippa, relatives, close friends, Areius, Maecenas, physicians, and priests—all have passed. Then contemplate the broader picture, not just the demise of one individual, but the extinction of an entire lineage, like the Pompeii, and the epitaphs that read, "The last of his line." Think about the exertions of those before to ensure a successor, only to arrive at the inevitability of an ultimate successor. Lastly, ponder on the extinction of an entire lineage.

It is your responsibility to manage your life with integrity in every single action; if each action fulfills its role to the best of its ability, be satisfied; no one can prevent you from ensuring that every act fulfills its duty. Yet, you may object that external circumstances will interfere. However, such circumstances cannot prevent you from acting with justice, moderation, and thoughtfulness. And if some outside force is indeed obstructed, by accepting the obstruction and willingly shifting your focus to what is permissible, a new avenue for action is immediately presented to you—one that is in harmony with the order we are discussing.

Accept wealth or success without conceit; and be prepared to release it without distress.

Consider this: if you have seen a severed hand, a foot, or a head, isolated from the rest of the body, you can grasp how a person who is dissatisfied with fate, who isolates himself from community, or who engages in divisive actions, becomes like those severed parts. If you have distanced yourself from the unity that nature intended—for you were created to be a part of it, but you have chosen to sever yourself—remember this gracious gift: you have the ability to rejoin. Nature has not granted this to any other part once it has been cut off and separated; it cannot reattach on its own. Reflect on the generosity with which humanity has been favored: not only has it been given the ability to avoid disunion from the whole, but even after separation, it has been granted the chance to return, to reunify, and to reclaim its place as part of the larger whole.

Just as the universal nature has endowed every rational being with all the capacities it possesses, we too have been granted the ability to utilize obstacles to our advantage. As the universe transforms and aligns everything that resists it into its predetermined order, incorporating such elements into itself, so too can the rational being turn every impediment into useful resource, adapting it for its intended use.

Do not allow yourself to be overwhelmed by contemplating the entirety of your life. Do not allow your mind to be preoccupied with all the potential hardships that may arise; instead, ask yourself in each instance, "What is unbearable or insurmountable about this situation?" You will likely find yourself reluctant to admit that there is anything. Moreover, remember that it is not the future or the past that troubles you, but only the present moment. And this can be minimized to something quite manageable if you set boundaries for it and reprimand your mind if it struggles to cope with even this limited scope.

Consider the absurdity: do Panthea or Pergamus linger by Verus's tomb? Do Chaurias or Diotimus keep vigil at Hadrian's resting place? It would be absurd. Even if they did, would the departed be aware? And if the departed had awareness, would it bring them joy? And even if it did provide some sense of pleasure, would that grant them eternity? Was it not inevitable by fate that they would age and eventually pass away? What would be the course of action for those remaining once they, too, had gone? All that remains in the end is decay and the remnants within a corpse.

"If you have clear vision, observe and judge wisely," advises the philosopher.

In the nature of the rational being, I find no quality that stands in conflict with justice; however, I do perceive a quality that challenges the pursuit of pleasure, and that quality is self-control.

If you remove your negative judgment about what seems to cause you pain, you will be at peace. - Who is this 'you'? - It is reason. - But I am not merely reason. - Even so, let your reasoning mind not disturb itself. Should any other part of you suffer, let that part hold its own opinion about its suffering.

An obstruction to the senses is detrimental to an animal's nature. Similarly, a block to its impulses is harmful. And for plants, there is another type of hindrance that is equally damaging. Therefore, anything that impedes the intellect is harmful to a rational nature.

Apply this to yourself. Are you affected by pain or pleasure? The senses will handle that. Have you encountered resistance in your pursuit? If you were working towards your goal without reservation, then indeed, this obstacle is harmful to you as a rational being. But considering the normal course of events, you are neither harmed nor hindered. Moreover, the faculties of the mind are not typically obstructed by others, for they are untouched by fire, iron, tyranny, or insults. Once the mind maintains its spherical form, it remains unaltered.

It is not appropriate for me to cause myself distress, for I have never intentionally caused distress to anyone else.

What brings joy varies from person to person. However, my joy comes from maintaining the integrity of my governing principle, without rejecting any person or the events that occur to people, but observing and accepting everything with open eyes and utilizing each according to its worth.

Make the most of the present moment for yourself; for those who seek fame after death should remember that future generations will be just like those they cannot tolerate now; and all are mortal. Why should it matter to you if future generations speak one way or another, or hold this or that view about you?

Take me and place me wherever you wish; there I will keep my inner divinity at peace, that is, content, if it can sense and act in accordance with its nature. Is a mere change of environment reason enough for my soul to become distressed and worsen, to become contracted, frightened, or intimidated? And what could possibly be a sufficient reason for such a reaction?

Nothing can happen to a person that is not a natural human occurrence, nor to an ox that is not in the nature of oxen, nor to a vine that is not in the nature of vines, nor to a stone that is not characteristic of stones. If, then, everything that happens does so according to its nature, why complain? The common nature of things brings about nothing that you cannot endure.

If you are troubled by something external, it is not the circumstance itself that upsets you, but rather your own judgment of it. And it is within your power to erase that judgment immediately. If something within your own attitude causes you distress, what prevents you from altering your perception? And if you are pained because you are not doing something which you believe to be right, why do you not choose to act rather than lament? - Is there an insurmountable obstacle in your path? - Then do not grieve, for its failure to be accomplished is not within your control. - If you believe life is not worth living if this cannot be achieved, then depart life serenely, just as one who dies in the midst of vigorous activity, content with the existence he has led and accepting of the barriers he encounters.

Remember that the ruling part of the mind is unconquerable when it gathers itself together, is content with itself, and does not undertake any action unwillingly, even if it resists out of sheer defiance. What will its power be, then, when it makes a judgment using reason and deliberate choice? Therefore, a mind free from passions is a fortress, for there is no stronghold more secure for a person to take refuge in and thereafter remain unassailable. One who has not recognized this is unenlightened, but one who does recognize it and yet does not seek this sanctuary is miserable.

Say no more to yourself than what the initial reports suggest. Suppose it is reported to you that someone has spoken ill of you. This has been reported; however, it has not been reported that you have been harmed. I observe that my child is ill. That I see; but whether he is in peril, I do not see. Therefore, stick with the initial appearances and add nothing more from within, and thus nothing adverse will befall you. Or rather, if you are to add anything, do so as someone who is fully informed about the nature of the world's occurrences.

If a cucumber is bitter, discard it. If there are thorns on the path, avoid them. That is sufficient. Do not question why such things exist in the world. A person who understands nature would laugh at such a complaint, just as a carpenter or a shoemaker would laugh if you complained about the shavings and offcuts in their workshops. They have a place to dispose of their waste, and the universe has an even more remarkable ability. Although it has no outside space to discard waste, nature ingeniously transforms what decays, ages, and becomes superfluous back into itself, creating new things from the same material, thus needing no external resources nor a dumping ground. It is self-sufficient in space, material, and process.

Do not be lethargic in your actions, nor disorganized in your speech. Do not let your thoughts wander aimlessly. Avoid internal turmoil and external spillage. In your life, be not so consumed by activity that you have no time for relaxation.

Imagine people are trying to kill you, dismember you, curse you. What can these actions do to prevent your mind from maintaining its purity, wisdom, sobriety, and fairness? Consider a clear and pure spring: if someone curses it, the spring continues to flow with drinkable water. If they throw mud or dirt into it, it will soon disperse and cleanse them away, remaining untainted. How can you maintain a perpetual spring within yourself and not just a temporary well? By continually shaping yourself towards freedom coupled with contentment, simplicity, and humility.

One who is ignorant of the nature of the universe is also unaware of his place within it. Likewise, if he does not understand the purpose of the universe's existence, he cannot comprehend who he is or the essence of the universe. Someone failing to grasp any of these concepts cannot even articulate the purpose of his own existence. What, then, can be said of the person who seeks or shuns the accolades of those who give praise, when they themselves do not understand where they are or who they are?

Why would you desire praise from someone who condemns himself several times every hour? Would you be eager to please someone who is discontent with himself? Can one truly be content if he regrets almost everything he does?

Let not your breath be the only thing that moves in unison with the surrounding air, but also let your intellect align with the universal mind that encompasses all. For the one willing to attune himself, the divine intelligence is as pervasive and accessible in all parts as the air is for those who breathe.

In the grand scheme, evil does not damage the universe; and specifically, one man's evil does not harm another. It is only detrimental to the person who harbors it and who can choose to rid himself of it whenever he decides.

The free will of another is as inconsequential to my own freedom as his breath and body. Although we are created to interact with one another, the governing part of each person has its distinct function. If this were not so, the wrongdoing of another could affect me, which is not the intention of the divine, lest my happiness be at the mercy of another's actions.

The sun seems to spread out in all directions, yet it does not dissipate; this spreading is simply its rays extending. We call them 'extensions' because they stretch out. By observing sunlight streaming through a narrow slit into a dark room, one sees how light extends straight ahead, splitting around any object that blocks its path, without losing its integrity. In the same way, our understanding should radiate outwards—not as a spillage, but as a deliberate reach, encountering obstacles without aggression or collapse, but with a steady presence that illuminates what it touches. A body that does not open itself up will miss out on this light.

Those who dread death are either afraid of losing all sensation or experiencing a new kind. If you cease to feel, you will not experience any harm; if you encounter a new sensation, you will simply exist in a different state, but you will continue to live.

We are here to interact with one another. Either instruct them or learn to tolerate them.

Just as an arrow flies, so does the mind. Whether it is proceeding with caution or engaging in deep thought, the mind moves straight towards its target.

Engage with the governing part of each person's mind, and allow them to connect with yours.

Workbook Exercises
Book VIII

E **mpathy for Others**

Marcus emphasizes understanding the actions of others through empathy. Reflect on a recent conflict or misunderstanding. How can empathy toward the other person's perspective change your view of the situation?

The Common Good

Marcus often reflects on acting for the common good. Consider your actions and decisions: how do they contribute to the welfare of others? Are there areas where you can improve?

Inner Strength

Reflect on the source of your inner strength. How do you cultivate resilience in the face of life's challenges, as Marcus suggests?

Purposeful Actions

Marcus advises that actions should be purposeful and not random. Reflect on your daily activities: are they driven by purpose? How can you ensure your actions align with your life's purpose?

Mortality and Legacy

Contemplate your mortality as Marcus often does. What legacy do you hope to leave behind, and how does this shape your actions and priorities now?

Meditations: Book IX

Whoever acts unjustly also acts irreverently. This is because the universal nature has created rational beings for the purpose of mutual assistance, to act according to merit and not for harm. Those who go against this intent commit an offense against the supreme divinity. Similarly, the one who lies is also irreverent, because the universal nature corresponds to the essence of things that exist, and these things are interconnected with all that is brought into existence. Moreover, this universal nature is synonymous with truth, which is the fundamental cause of all that is true. Hence, anyone who deliberately lies commits an irreverent act, as he unjustly causes deception; and even if one lies unintentionally, he is still at odds with the universal nature, disrupting the world's order by opposing what is true. This opposition arises when a person, through neglecting his natural abilities, can no longer discern falsehood from truth.

The one who regards pleasure as a good and pain as an evil is also guilty of irreverence. Such a person will inevitably criticize the universal nature for its distribution of outcomes, arguing that it often bestows pleasures upon the wicked and inflict pains upon the virtuous, contrary to what they deserve. Moreover, anyone who dreads pain may also fear certain aspects of the world's unfolding events, and this too constitutes irreverence. Similarly, someone who chases pleasure will not refrain from committing injustices, which is clearly irreverent.

Regarding those aspects to which the universal nature is indifferent—for it would not have created them if it valued one over the other—those who wish to align with nature should adopt an identical stance and be impartial. When it comes to pain and pleasure, or death and life, or dishonor and honor—elements that the universal nature uses without preference—anyone who does not meet these with equanimity is unmistakably behaving irreverently. By saying the universal nature employs these without preference, I mean that these conditions are common to all beings, both those existing as part of a continuous sequence and those who emerge subsequently, through an initial act of Providence. This act initiated the current order of things from a certain beginning, envisaging specific principles for the things that were to come into existence, and determining the forces that would give rise to life, to change, and to successive generations.

The most fortunate condition for a person would be to leave this world having never experienced deceit, pretense, extravagance, or arrogance. However, the next best fate is to depart life having grown weary of these vices. Have you not yet resolved to abandon wrongdoing, even after recognizing its harmful effects? Remember, the decay of the intellect is a far graver affliction than any deterioration of the air we breathe. The latter may harm living creatures in their animal aspect, but the former is a calamity for humans in their essence as rational beings.

Embrace the concept of death as part of nature's will, just as natural as being young or old, growing or maturing, having teeth or white hair, procreating, bearing children, and all other natural events that life's seasons bring. It is the mark of a person who lives with mindfulness to neither dismiss death with indifference nor to await it with impatience or disdain, but to accept it as one of nature's processes. Just as you anticipate the moment a child is born, so too should you prepare for the moment your soul shall leave this body. And if you need a more commonplace solace to reach your heart, consider the circumstances and the company you are about to leave. There is no justification for feeling animosity towards people, for it is your responsibility to care for and to be patient with them; however, it is also true that your departure will be from those who do not share your values and principles. This lack of shared principles could be the only thing that might make us cling to life – the chance to live with those who align with our own principles. But when you see the strife caused by the disharmony of those living together, you might find yourself thinking, 'Let death come quickly, before I too am drawn into such discord and forget who I am.'

He who commits an injustice harms himself, for in doing so, he becomes corrupt.

It is not only the person who performs an action that can be unjust but also he who neglects to act when he ought to.

Your current state of mind, based on understanding, your actions aimed at the common good, and your acceptance of whatever occurs—these are sufficient for a good life.

Eliminate fanciful thoughts; restrain your desires; put an end to your cravings; maintain your inner guiding principle in its rightful authority.

In creatures without reason, a single life force is spread amongst many. Yet, in beings endowed with reason, there is a share in one collective intellect. Just as we are all connected to the same earth from which earthly things come and are illuminated by the same light, we all share the same breath of life—those of us with the power of sight and all who are endowed with life.

All entities that share a common element naturally gravitate towards similar entities. Earthly substances combine with the earth, liquids flow together, and aerial substances seek each other out, often requiring separation by force. Fire, inherently upward-reaching due to its elemental nature, is easily united with any fire present, as it ignites substances with dryness readily, for there's little to obstruct its combustion.

Likewise, beings endowed with the common rational nature are drawn even more strongly to what is akin to them. Just as they are superior to other entities, they also exhibit a greater propensity for union with their like. In irrational animals, we observe colonies of bees, herds of livestock, the raising of chicks, and a semblance of affection, for they possess souls and show a unifying force that appears stronger than anything manifested in plants or inanimate nature. In rational beings, this force gives rise to societies, friendships, families, and assemblies; and it is seen in the formal agreements of peace and truce in conflicts. Even among superior beings that are separate from one another, such as the stars, there is a kind of unity.

This capacity to ascend and resonate, even across distances, suggests a natural sympathy. However, it is only intelligent beings that seem to have forgotten this inherent attraction to one another, not readily displaying this tendency to coalesce. Yet, despite their efforts to stay apart, they are inevitably drawn together by the overpowering force of their nature. Observe this phenomenon, and you will notice that it is rarer to find an earthly substance that does not interact with its kind than a human being completely isolated from others.

Every entity, including humans, deities, and the cosmos itself, yields its own fruit when the time is right. This is true even if we more commonly use the term "fruit" for the produce of plants like the grapevine. But let's not get caught up in terminology. Reason yields its own kind of fruit — benefits for both the individual and for others. It also gives rise to more reasoned thoughts and actions.

If it is within your power, gently guide those who err back onto the right path through education. If that's not possible, remember that you're granted the patience to tolerate them. The gods also show leniency towards such individuals and often aid them in gaining health, wealth, and esteem, such is their benevolence. And you can do the same — unless something is preventing you?

Do not toil as if you are miserable, or seeking pity or admiration. Instead, align your will solely with the objective of acting and restraining yourself according to the demands of communal rationality.

Today, I have extricated myself from all distress, or rather, I have discarded it, for it was within me, in my own perceptions, not outside.

All things are repetitive in experience, fleeting in duration, and insignificant in substance. The current state of affairs is as it was in the times of those who have passed away.

Objects exist independently, with no awareness or capacity for judgment about themselves. It is the mind that assesses and understands them.

It is not in being passive, but in taking action, that the rational and social creature finds its misfortune or fortune, and similarly, its moral character or lack thereof is defined by action, not inaction.

For a stone that has been hurled skyward, there is no harm in falling, nor is there any benefit in having been lifted.

Look deeply into the motives of people, and you will understand the nature of the authorities you fear — and see what kind of judges they are over their own actions.

Everything is in flux, and you are no exception, undergoing constant change and decay, and the entire universe is as well.

It is your responsibility to leave another person's misdeeds where they lie.

The end of activity, the stilling of motion and opinion, akin to their own demise, is not to be deemed harmful. Consider your own life's journey — your childhood, your youth, your adult years, and old age; in each phase, the transition was like a small death. Is there reason to fear such transitions? Reflect on your life during your grandfather's time, then under your mother's care, and finally under your father's guidance. As you recognize the many shifts and endings, ask yourself, is there truly anything to fear? Similarly, the conclusion and transformation at the end of your life should not be feared.

Make haste to evaluate your own guiding principle, the principle governing the universe, and that of those around you: refine your own to ensure it is just; understand the universe's to comprehend your part in it; and discern your neighbor's to grasp whether his actions were done in ignorance or knowledge, and to acknowledge that his rational nature is related to yours.

Since you are part of a larger community, ensure that each of your actions contributes to this communal life. Any act that does not directly or indirectly serve a communal purpose disrupts the unity of your life and is akin to an act of rebellion, just as a single individual's dissent can disrupt the harmony of a collective assembly.

The squabbles and play of children, the carrying of lifeless bodies — all of life is like this, akin to the macabre displays in tombs that remind us starkly of our mortality.

Inspect the form of an object, separate it from its material substance, and then consider it in isolation. Afterwards, evaluate the span, the longest duration such a specific form is likely to last.

You have faced endless troubles because you were not satisfied with your rational faculty when it performed its natural functions. But let that be in the past.

When someone criticizes or despises you, or people speak ill of you, reach out to their souls. Delve within and see what sort of people they really are. You'll find there's no need to be troubled by their opinions of you. Nonetheless, you should be kindly disposed towards them, for by nature they are your companions. And the gods assist them in various ways, with dreams and omens, to achieve what they value.

The cycles of the cosmos are unchanging, waxing and waning through the ages. If the divine mind initiates each specific event, then find contentment in the outcomes of its will; or if the first motion cascades into all subsequent events, accept the sequence that unfolds; or if primal elements are the foundation of all, then this is the nature of reality. In essence, if there is a deity, all is in order; and if random chance dominates, do not be ruled by it yourself.

Soon, we will all be interred beneath the soil, which will itself undergo transformation, and the products of this change will continue in an endless cycle of transformation. Anyone who contemplates the relentless succession of changes, each rapidly giving way to the next, will regard all perishable things with indifference.

The universal cause is akin to a torrential river of winter: it sweeps everything in its path. But consider how insignificant are those engrossed in political affairs, believing themselves to be philosophers — they are but trifles. So, do what is demanded of you by nature at this moment. Act on your own initiative, without concern for observation or recognition; do not hold out for an ideal society like Plato's Republic. Rejoice even in the smallest success and do not deem it trivial. For who has the power to change the opinions of others? Without changing their minds, what else remains but the servitude of those who toil under a facade of obedience? Reflect on historical figures like Alexander, Philip, and Demetrius of Phalerum — let them assess whether they discerned what nature demands and adapted themselves to its call. But if they merely played roles in life's tragedies, no one has decreed that I must emulate them. The task of philosophy is straightforward and unassuming; do not lure me into inaction and vanity.

From a higher perspective, observe the multitudes of people, their elaborate rituals, the myriad journeys across tumultuous and serene seas, the divergences in the lives of those born, who coexist and eventually pass away. Reflect on the existence led by ancient peoples, those who will live in the future, and those in distant lands unknown to you, many of whom are unaware of your name, and many more who will quickly forget it. Consider how those who might now commend you will soon find fault, and recognize that neither fame after death, nor current renown, nor anything else holds true value.

Embrace tranquility when faced with disturbances sparked by external events; and exercise justice in actions propelled by internal decisions, specifically those that result in societal engagement, for this aligns with your inherent nature.

You have the capacity to dismiss many of the inconveniences that unsettle you, as they exist solely in your perception. By embracing the vastness of the universe in your thoughts, by pondering the infinity of time, and by recognizing the fleeting nature of each individual transformation — how brief the interval from emergence to dissolution, and the boundless expanses of time both before birth and after demise — you will secure for yourself a significant expanse of serenity.

Everything you observe will soon decay, and those who witness its disintegration will not be far behind. The one who departs at the zenith of old age and the one who departs prematurely will eventually converge in the same state.

Reflect upon the guiding principles of these individuals, the pursuits that occupy them, the motives for their affections and respects. Envision their souls exposed in their vulnerability. When they suppose they inflict damage with their criticism or bestow benefit with their praise, consider the naivety of such beliefs.

Loss is merely a form of transformation, a process in which the universal nature finds joy. This natural order has perpetuated all things admirably from eternity and will continue in this manner forever. What then can you infer? That all has always been fraught with misfortune, that no divine being has had the power to amend these conditions, and that the world is fated to eternal suffering and incapacity for improvement?

Consider the base nature of all elements: water, dust, bones, grime; or on the other hand, majestic marble, earth's hardened lumps; gold and silver, mere sediments; fabrics, but strands of hair; and purple dye, simply blood. Everything else mirrors this essence. The breath of life, too, is just as transient, ever transforming from one state to another.

Let go of this tiresome existence, the grumbling, and the trivial antics. Why be perturbed? What is so startling or new? What shakes your composure? Is it the shape of things? Observe it closely. Or the substance? Examine that as well. Beyond these, there is nothing more. It is time now to turn to the gods with simplicity and improvement in mind. It makes little difference whether you scrutinize these matters for centuries or mere days.

If someone has committed an offense, the burden is theirs alone. Yet it's possible no wrongdoing has occurred.

All that exists is either the offspring of a singular, intelligent origin, united as one entity, and a part should not complain against what benefits the whole; or there is nothing but atoms, chaos, and disintegration. So why be disturbed? Ask your guiding spirit: Are you deceased, corrupted, deceitful, have you degenerated into a brute, mingling and grazing with the herd?

The gods either possess strength or they do not. If they are powerless, why petition them? But if they are potent, why not request that they grant you the ability not to fear what you fear, not to crave what you desire, or not to suffer from what pains you, instead of pleading for these events not to occur? For if they can collaborate with humans, they surely can assist in these areas. But you may argue that the gods have placed these things within our control. Then isn't it preferable to exercise our power freely rather than to yearn for what's beyond our grasp in a servile manner? And who is to say the gods don't support us in matters that are within our control? Start to pray for such strength and observe the outcome. Let one man pray to be with a woman; you should pray not to have the desire. Let another pray for release from something; you should pray not to wish for that release. And where one prays not to lose a child, you should pray not to fear losing him. Ultimately, redirect your prayers in this manner and witness the results.

Epicurus, renowned for his teachings on pleasure and pain, highlights an admirable approach to adversity and illness. His focus remained steadfast on the nature of things, the workings of the universe, and how the mind can maintain tranquility amidst the 'movements' of the flesh—that is, despite physical pain or discomfort.

To follow Epicurus's example is to continue engaging with philosophy, or your guiding principles, regardless of the situation—be it sickness or other challenges. Philosophy here is more than academic discourse; it is the art of living. It's about persisting in the pursuit of one's proper good and the exercise of rational faculties to remain undisturbed by external circumstances.

This approach suggests that even in times of distress, one need not dwell on the affliction, allowing it to become the center of conversation or thought. Instead, it's about redirecting attention to maintain mental composure and continuing to engage in meaningful dialogue or activities that align with one's understanding of nature and existence.

By not dramatizing the situation or giving it more attention than it requires, one does not allow the 'physicians'—literal or metaphorical—to don their 'solemn looks', meaning one does not succumb to the external show of the situation but keeps a balanced and happy life. It's a call to focus on what is essential—the task at hand and the means by which it is accomplished.

Epicurus's attitude invites us to consider how we address our own challenges and engage with others, especially in difficult times. It emphasizes the importance of keeping a clear mind and purpose, continuing to live according to one's principles, and not getting caught up in either our own troubles or in trivial conversations. This way, we can aim to live well and contentedly, regardless of our circumstances.

When you find yourself aggrieved by someone's disgraceful behavior, consider promptly: Can it be that there are no such men of shame in the world? It cannot be. Thus, do not wish for the impossible. This individual is necessarily one of those people who are bound to exist in the world. This realization should guide your thoughts not only about the deceitful, the unfaithful, and all who do harm, but also toward a gentler attitude to each person as an individual. Recognize the virtue nature has instilled in humanity to counteract every misdeed; for instance, she offers gentleness as a remedy against ignorance. Moreover, you have the opportunity to educate those who have erred; for every person who does wrong has simply missed their true aim and lost their way.

Consider where you have truly been harmed. You'll see that none of those who anger you have worsened your mind; only your own thoughts can do that. What harm is there if an untaught person acts according to their lack of knowledge? Perhaps it is you who should fault yourself for not foreseeing their mistake when you had the rational capacity to anticipate it, yet you forgot and are now surprised by their error. When you criticize someone for being disloyal or ungrateful, reflect on yourself. The error clearly lies with you, whether you trusted someone untrustworthy or if you gave your kindness conditionally, not purely for the sake of being kind, or in such a way as to expect a benefit in return. When you have been of service to another, why seek recompense? Are you not satisfied having acted in accordance with your nature? It would be as absurd as the eyes wanting reward for seeing or the feet for walking. Just as each organ functions according to its purpose and benefits thereby, so too, when you act generously or promote the common good, you are simply fulfilling your nature and receiving what is rightfully yours.

Workbook Exercises
Book IX

Consistency of Values

Marcus emphasizes the importance of living consistently with your values. Reflect on your core values. Are your daily actions in alignment with these values, and if not, how can you bring them into greater harmony?

Mindfulness of Speech

Marcus advises us to speak only what is necessary and true. Think about recent conversations. How might this guidance change the way you communicate?

Perception of Pleasure and Pain

Consider your perceptions of pleasure and pain. Reflect on a recent experience of each. How do your attitudes toward these sensations influence your happiness and peace of mind?

Universal Connectedness

Reflect on Marcus' notion of universal connectedness. How does this idea influence your feelings of responsibility toward others and the world?

Harmony Within the Self

Marcus emphasizes the need for inner harmony. Reflect on aspects of your inner life that feel in conflict. How might you work toward a more harmonious state of being?

Meditations: Book X

W ill you, my soul, ever be noble, straightforward, pure, and completely trans-
parent, more so than the body that encloses you? Will you ever attain a state
of deep affection and contentment? Will you be fulfilled, lacking nothing, not yearning
for anything more, neither for the company of creatures nor for objects to indulge in
pleasures? Will you cease to long for more time to enjoy life, or for a different place, a
better climate, or the companionship of people with whom you could live in harmony?
Can you be content with your current lot, satisfied with your surroundings, and persuade
yourself that you possess everything you need, understanding it is from the gods, and that
all is well as long as it suits their will, whatever they may bestow upon you to preserve
a perfect, living being—a being that is good, just, and beautiful, one that generates and
unites all things, and holds and encompasses everything that breaks down to give rise to
others like itself? Will you ever become such a person who lives in harmony with both
gods and men, without complaining about them or being subject to their criticism?

Consider what your nature demands, to the extent that you are governed solely by it:
then do it and embrace it, as long as it doesn't deteriorate your condition as a living being.

Then, you must consider what your nature demands as you are a living being. Allow
yourself all this, as long as your nature, as a rational creature, isn't degraded by it. And
since a rational creature is also a social being by nature, adhere to these principles and
concern yourself with nothing else.

Everything that occurs will do so in a manner that you are either naturally equipped to
handle or not. If it is something within your natural capacity to endure, do not complain
but endure it as you are meant to. If it is not something you are naturally able to bear, do
not complain, for it will pass as it consumes you. Remember that you are naturally able

to bear anything that depends on your personal judgment to find bearable and tolerable, by considering it to be either in your interest or your duty to do so.

If someone is in error, kindly instruct them and point out their mistake. If you cannot do this, then fault yourself, or rather, do not fault yourself at all.

Whatever happens to you has been destined for you from the beginning of time, and the network of causes was eternally weaving the fabric of your existence, along with all that happens to you.

Whether the universe is a random assembly of atoms or a structured entity governed by nature, it is essential to acknowledge that I am a part of the greater whole which nature oversees. Additionally, I share a deep connection with elements that are similar to me. With this awareness, as a component of the whole, I will not be dissatisfied with any of the roles allotted to me by the entirety, because what benefits the whole cannot be detrimental to its parts. The whole comprises only that which is beneficial to it, a notion common to all beings, but the nature of the universe is also such that it cannot be forced by any external factor to produce something harmful to itself. Bearing in mind that I am a fragment of such a system, I shall be at peace with everything that transpires. Furthermore, since I am closely linked to the elements akin to me, I will not engage in anti-social acts but will aim to unite with my counterparts, steering my endeavors toward our mutual benefit and away from what is adverse. If these principles are followed, life ought to flow smoothly, much like the life of a citizen who contributes positively to the community, remains in harmony with what society bestows upon him, and thus experiences a contented existence.

All things that are part of the universe, which naturally fall within its scope, must inevitably undergo change and perish, though 'perish' should be understood as transformation rather than destruction. If such change and decay were inherently harmful and necessary, then the whole could not maintain its integrity and goodness, as its parts would be in a constant state of demise and subject to various forms of destruction. It would be absurd to think that nature intentionally causes harm to its own components, making them inherently prone to misfortune and destined to succumb to it, or that such events occur without nature's awareness. These assumptions are hard to believe.

Even if we discard the notion of Nature as an active force and simply consider these occurrences as 'natural', it remains illogical to accept that the parts of the whole are naturally changeable, yet feel surprise or distress when changes occur as though they were unnatural. Moreover, the decomposition of things is a return to the elements from which they originated. There is a dissolution of the compounds back to their basic elements, or a transformation of the solid to the earthy, the airy to the aerial, rejoining these elements to the universal logic of nature, whether through periodic conflagrations or through ceaseless transformation.

Do not presume that the solid and airy elements that constitute you have been yours since birth. In truth, they were assimilated quite recently, from the nourishment and air you have taken in just days ago. Thus, what changes is not the essence that your mother gave birth to, but what has been subsequently accumulated. Even if it appears that what your mother brought forth is closely bound to the mutable aspect of your being, this does not fundamentally challenge the argument presented.

When you adopt the virtues of being good, modest, truthful, rational, even-tempered, and great-hearted, ensure that you live up to these qualities and swiftly return to them if you falter. Bear in mind that to be 'Rational' means to apply discerning thought to every matter and to shun carelessness; 'Even-tempered' signifies the willing embrace of what nature has allotted to you; 'Great-hearted' is to lift your intellect above the pulls of physical pleasure or pain, the allure of reputation, the fear of death, and all such ephemeral concerns. If you embody these virtues for their own sake, not seeking acclaim, you will transform and embark upon a new way of living. To cling to your former ways, subject to degradation and disarray, is akin to those maimed gladiators who, though maimed and bleeding, plead to be spared until tomorrow, only to face the same brutal combat.

Cling, then, to these noble titles, and if you can persist in them, live as if you've been transported to a blissful retreat. But should you find yourself slipping, courageously retreat to a place where you can sustain them, or even depart from life, not in anger or sorrow, but with serenity, freedom, and dignity, having achieved at least this one worthy deed.

To keep these virtues in mind, it helps to remember the gods, who desire not flattery but the betterment of all rational beings. Remember that each being has its purpose: as a fig tree produces figs, a dog acts as a dog, a bee produces honey, and a man must fulfill the role of a man.

Mockery, conflict, shock, numbness, and servitude will gradually erode your sacred principles. How often do you conjure up notions or overlook matters without considering nature? Yet, it is your responsibility to observe and act in such a way that you hone the skill to manage situations effectively, cultivate a reflective mindset, and retain self-assuredness from your understanding of each individual matter—displaying it subtly, without ostentation. When will you value simplicity, solemnity, and a comprehensive understanding of each thing: its essence, its role in the cosmos, its destined lifespan, its components, its ownership, and who has the right to bestow or to take it away?

A spider takes pride in ensnaring a fly, just as others take pride in capturing a hare, snaring a small fish, hunting wild boars, trapping bears, or conquering Sarmatians. If you consider their underlying motives, aren't these all acts of theft?

Embrace a contemplative approach to perceive the transformation of things into one another, devote constant attention to this practice, and immerse yourself in this aspect of philosophy. For such contemplation is uniquely suited to foster a magnanimous spirit. The person who embraces this view has transcended the physical form, recognizing that soon, at an undetermined time, he must depart from the company of others and leave all earthly things behind. He commits fully to righteous action in all he undertakes, and in all life's happenings, he acquiesces to the will of the cosmos. Regarding what others might say, think, or do against him, he remains indifferent, finding solace in two things alone: acting honorably in his current deeds and being content with his present lot. He eschews all distractions and frenetic activities, seeking only to adhere to the righteous path prescribed by law, thus aligning himself with the divine.

Why fear suspicion when you have the ability to seek what should be done? If your path is clear, proceed with satisfaction and do not look back. If uncertain, halt and consult the best advisors. When faced with obstacles, continue with your abilities, giving due thought, and adhering to what seems fair. Striving for this ideal is the goal; even if you fail, let it be in the pursuit of it. The one who follows reason closely is simultaneously calm, active, content, and composed.

Upon waking, ask yourself if it matters whether someone else performs acts of justice and righteousness. It makes no difference.

Surely, you recall those who pompously dispense their praise or criticism are no different in their private moments. Remember their actions, their avoidance, their desires, and how they corrupt their most valuable part—their ability to be loyal, modest, truthful, lawful, and thus attain true well-being.

To Nature, who bestows and reclaims all, the enlightened and humble person says, "Grant what you will; reclaim what you will." Not with arrogance, but with compliance and contentment.

Your remaining time is brief. Live as though on a mountain; it matters not whether here or there, if one lives as a citizen of the world. Let others see and know a true person living naturally. If they can't stand him, it is better he is eliminated than live untruthfully.

Cease talking about what a good person should be and simply be one.

Reflect on the entirety of time and substance, understanding that all individual things are as insignificant as a fig seed in the scale of the universe, and fleeting as the twist of a drill.

Observe all that exists, recognizing that it is already in decay, changing, disintegrating, or designed by nature to perish.

Reflect on human nature during daily acts such as eating, sleeping, procreating, relieving themselves, and other such activities. Think also of their demeanor when they exert authority or express anger from their positions of power. Not long ago, these same individuals were subservient to others for various reasons, and soon enough, consider what their state will be.

What serves the well-being of each entity is that which the universal nature bestows upon it, at the precise time it does so.

Just as the earth welcomes rain and the vast sky loves, the universe is inclined to create what is about to come into existence. I thus align myself with the universe, embracing what it produces with love. Is it not also true that everything has its own natural propensity to emerge?

You either live here and have grown accustomed to it, you're leaving by your own choice, or you're passing away having fulfilled your role. There is nothing more. Therefore, take heart.

Remember this clearly: this place is like any other. What happens here is the same as what happens on a mountain, by the sea, or anywhere you choose to be. As Plato observed, life within a city's walls is akin to life in a shepherd's fold on a mountain.

Ask yourself: What is my guiding principle at this moment? What character am I shaping it to have? For what purpose am I using it? Is it devoid of comprehension? Has it become detached from the communal life? Is it so entwined with the flesh that it moves in unison with it?

One who disobeys the law is like a slave who has fled from their master, for the law is our master. And anyone who experiences grief, anger, or fear is reacting against what is decreed by the ruler of all, who is the embodiment of Law and designates what is appropriate for each. Thus, the one who is afraid, aggrieved, or enraged is like a runaway.

A man plants a seed in a womb and then leaves; another force takes over, nurtures it, and a child is formed from such simple beginnings. Similarly, a child ingests food, and yet another force converts it into perception, motion, life, vigor, and more—how varied and remarkable! Observe these subtle processes and recognize the power behind them, just as you acknowledge the force that moves things up and down, not seen with the eyes but equally evident.

Always bear in mind that things as they are now were the same in the past, and they will recur in the future. Visualize the complete dramas and scenes of the same nature that you have experienced or learned from ancient history—for instance, the courts of Hadrian, Antoninus, Philip, Alexander, and Croesus. All these were similar spectacles to what we witness now, merely with different players.

Consider anyone who is troubled or dissatisfied with their circumstances as akin to a pig that resists and squeals when it is about to be sacrificed. Similarly, think of the person who silently laments in bed over the constraints that bind us. Remember, only rational beings have the privilege of accepting willingly what comes to pass; for all others, acceptance is a compulsion.

In the face of every action you undertake, take a moment to question whether the concept of death is fearsome because it robs you of these experiences.

When you find fault in another, immediately reflect on your own missteps, such as valuing money, pleasure, or a measure of fame too highly. This introspection can help dissipate your ire, especially if you consider that the other person is acting under compulsion—what else could they do? Or, if it's within your power, help remove the compulsion from them.

Upon encountering someone like Satyron the Socratic, think of Eutyches or Hymen; when you see Euphrates, bring to mind Eutychion or Silvanus; upon meeting Alciphron, think of Tropaeophorus; when you think of Xenophon, remember Crito or Severus; and when you consider yourself, think of any emperor. For each individual you meet, do the same. Then remind yourself: Where are these individuals now? They are nowhere or no one knows where. By doing this, you will come to view all human affairs as ephemeral and insignificant, especially if you consider that what has changed once will never be the same again through the endless span of time.

Why are you not at peace to journey through this brief life in a calm and orderly manner? What events and opportunities are you avoiding? For what are these events if not opportunities for your reasoning to practice, examining carefully the nature of what happens in life? Continue this practice until you fully assimilate these lessons, just as a strong stomach digests all it consumes, or as a bright fire transforms everything thrown into it into flames and light.

Let no one have the truth on their side when they claim that you lack simplicity or goodness. Let anyone who suggests this be speaking falsely, and know that being true to these virtues lies entirely within your control. Ask yourself, who has the power to prevent you from living with goodness and straightforwardness? Resolve to live only if you can live in this way; for reason itself dictates that a life without these virtues is not a life worth living.

Consider then, what actions or words are most in harmony with reason concerning the substance of our life. Whatever these actions or words may be, know that you have the power to execute or speak them, and do not entertain the notion that you are obstructed. Your lamentation will not cease until your mind finds that what is as delightful to the pleasure-seeker, you find in doing what aligns with human nature. For every man should see as a pleasure that which he can perform according to his own nature—and this is within his capacity wherever he is. A cylinder cannot move on its own, nor can water, fire, or any other element controlled by nature or an irrational impulse because they face numerous obstacles. Yet intelligence and reason have the capacity to navigate any opposition they encounter, operating in accordance with their nature and deliberate choice. Imagine the ease with which reason traverses all obstacles, as naturally as fire ascends or a stone falls, or a cylinder rolls down a slope—seek nothing beyond this. For other barriers only impact the body—which is in itself insensible—and do not truly cause suffering or damage unless the mind decides to perceive them as such. If they truly caused harm, then anyone who experienced it would become corrupt. However, when something with a specific nature is harmed, it deteriorates; whereas a person can become better and more commendable when they use such occurrences wisely. Lastly, bear in mind that nothing that does not harm the laws of the community can harm the citizen. And nothing harms the community that does not also harm the law and order it upholds; and none of the things we deem misfortunes do harm to the law. Therefore, that which does not harm the law harms neither the community nor the citizen within it.

For someone who has internalized profound truths, even the simplest directive can be enough to remind him to remain undisturbed by sorrow or fear. Consider this:

Like leaves that the wind disperses across the earth, so are the generations of men. Your own offspring are as leaves, as are those who clamor for trust and heap praises, or conversely, those who curse, secretly reproach, or mock. Likewise, are the individuals who will pass on one's legacy to future generations. All these emerge in their season, as a poet might say; they are then scattered by the wind, and in their place, the forest brings forth new leaves. Yet all things share a fleeting existence, and still, you chase or flee from them as if they were everlasting. In a brief span, you will shut your eyes in death, and soon another will mourn your passing.

A sound eye should be able to see all things within sight and not express a preference for only the green; this would be a sign of an eye that is unwell. Similarly, ears that hear and a nose that smells should be receptive to all they can sense. A healthy stomach should be indifferent to the variety of foods it processes, just as a mill grinds whatever grain it is given. In the same vein, a sound mind should be ready for whatever life brings. The mind that wishes only for the survival and praise of its children, or for universal acclaim for its deeds, is like an eye that only looks for greenery, or teeth that will only chew the softest morsels.

No person is so favored that, at the time of their death, there won't be someone nearby who is relieved at their passing. Even if the dying man were good and wise, there will likely be someone who thinks, "Finally, we can breathe a sigh of relief without this pedagogue among us." He might not have been overtly harsh, but his mere presence made us feel judged. This is often said about a decent person. Now, consider our own situation: there are plenty more reasons for people to wish us gone. Reflect on this as you approach death, and you'll find peace in the thought: "I'm leaving a life where even those for whom I've labored, for whose sake I've toiled and cared, are eager for me to go, perhaps in hopes of some small gain." Why cling to life under such circumstances? Yet, leave not with bitterness towards them, but with your character intact, maintaining kindness, benevolence, and gentleness—not feeling as though you're being torn away, but departing as one who dies a tranquil death, the soul willingly parting from the body. Nature joined you with others and now she separates you. If so, I leave as from relatives—not with resistance, but without struggle, for this too is in accordance with nature.

Make it a habit to ask yourself whenever someone does something, "What is their motive here?" But start with yourself; scrutinize your own motives first.

Always remember that the true essence, the life force within you, is your capacity for reasoning and your soul, not merely the physical shell that encases you and the appendages attached to it. They are comparable to tools, such as an axe bonded to the body, but without the directing force behind them, they are as useless as a weaver's shuttle, a writer's pen, or a charioteer's whip.

Workbook Exercises Book X

The Essence of Self

Marcus encourages focusing on the essence of one's character. Reflect on what defines you beyond your social roles and physical attributes. How can you nurture and express your true self more fully?

The Illusion of Control

Reflect on Marcus' assertion that many things are outside our control. Identify something you've tried to control but couldn't. How can letting go of this need for control bring you peace?

Personal Accountability

Marcus emphasizes the importance of self-examination and personal accountability. Reflect on your actions over the past week. Have they been aligned with your moral compass, and where can you take more responsibility?

Meditations: Book XI

T he rational soul has unique qualities: it has the capacity for self-perception, self-examination, and it shapes itself according to its will. The benefits of its endeavors are enjoyed by the soul itself, unlike the fruits of plants or the offspring of animals which are enjoyed by others. It achieves its purpose no matter when life may end. Unlike a play or dance that feels incomplete if interrupted, the rational soul regards every act as whole and complete, able to affirm, "I possess what is mine," at any point.

Moreover, the rational soul spans the vastness of the universe, explores the emptiness that encircles it, appreciates its structure, reaches into the boundless span of time, and recognizes the cyclic renewal of all things. It understands that future generations will witness no novelties, nor did the ancients see anything we have not; essentially, a person at forty, if insightful, has seen all that has been and all that will be, through the consistency of nature's patterns. Other attributes of the rational soul include love for one's fellow human beings, dedication to truth, modesty, and the principle that nothing is more valuable than itself, which is also a characteristic of Law. Hence, the reasoning of justice is indistinguishable from the principle of right reason.

You would diminish your esteem for songs, dances, and athletic contests if you analyzed the music note by note and questioned whether any single tone could overpower you—you would likely feel too embarrassed to admit it. Apply the same scrutiny to each step of a dance or each move in an athletic competition. In all matters other than virtue and virtuous actions, dissect them into their components to diminish their perceived value; employ this approach to all aspects of life.

Consider the soul that stands ready to part from the body at any moment, prepared for its potential extinguishment, scattering, or ongoing existence. Yet, this preparedness should stem from one's reasoned choice, not from stubborn defiance as seen with the Christians, but from a deliberate and dignified conviction that could convince others, eschewing melodrama.

If I have acted in the public interest, then I have received my reward. Let this principle endure in your thoughts, and let it drive you ceaselessly towards such benevolent action.

What is your profession? It is to be virtuous. And how can this be achieved if not by adhering to universal truths? Some about the cosmos, and some about human nature?

Originally, tragedies were staged to remind audiences of the common human experiences and to show them that such events are natural, encouraging them not to be distressed by real-life events similar to those depicted on the stage. We understand that things must happen in this way, and that people endure even when they lament their fate to the mountains, as the tragic characters do. And indeed, some playwrights express profound truths, such as:

"If the gods overlook me and my children,
There's a reason for that too."

And also:

"We mustn't rage against what happens."

And:

"Gather the harvest of life, as the field gathers its grain."

And there are many such sentiments.

Following tragedy came the old comedy, which spoke truth to power with its candid speech, serving as a reminder against arrogance. Diogenes, too, drew from these writers in his philosophical work.

Regarding the middle comedy that followed and the new comedy that emerged thereafter, sinking into mere theatrical gimmickry, consider their nature and their purpose. Even though they sometimes conveyed wise sayings, what was the ultimate intention behind such poetry and playwriting?

It becomes evident that there is no other state of life more conducive to the practice of philosophy than the one you find yourself in right now.

Just as a branch severed from its neighbor must also be inevitably separated from the entire tree, a man who distances himself from another also detaches from the larger community. While a branch is cut by another, a man can voluntarily isolate himself through animosity or rejection, not realizing he's severing ties with the collective society. However, we're afforded the opportunity by Zeus, the architect of our community, to reattach and contribute to the whole once more. Yet frequent separations make reintegration challenging, and the unity is never quite the same as that of the branch which has remained part of the tree since its inception.

As obstacles can't deter you when you act according to sound judgement, don't let them quench your goodwill either. Be vigilant in maintaining both your resolve in action and your compassion towards those who obstruct or unsettle you. It's a deficiency to succumb to irritation just as it is to falter in action or to be swayed by intimidation. Both types of failure represent a dereliction of duty—one born of fear, the other of estrangement from one's natural ally and friend.

No natural instinct is inferior to the practice of an art, for all arts are but imitations of nature's processes. Given this, the most supreme and encompassing nature, that of the universe, must surpass all artificial skill. The arts work on the lesser to benefit the greater, and so does the nature of the cosmos. This principle underlies justice, and upon justice rest all other virtues. Justice falters if we prioritize trivial things, or if we're prone to deception, negligence, and inconstancy.

If the things that disturb you don't come to you, it's often you who approaches them. So, let your judgement on these matters be still, and they will stand still too, and you won't be seen chasing after or fleeing from them.

The soul keeps its perfect form when it is neither stretched out towards something, retracted within, scattered, nor deflated, but is bathed in light, allowing it to perceive truth—the truth within all things and within itself.

Should someone look down upon me, that is for him to reckon with. As for me, my concern is to ensure I'm not found engaging in or expressing anything worthy of scorn. Should someone bear ill will towards me? That is their own issue. On my part, I shall remain kind and good-natured to all, always prepared to gently reveal to anyone their error, not with scorn or as a display of patience, but with dignity and sincerity, like the great Phocion—assuming his demeanor was not a facade. For what truly matters is the inner quality of our character; one should stand in the presence of the divine without resentment or grievance. What harm does it do you if you are now acting in harmony with your own nature, and content with what is presently required by the universal nature, given that you, as a human, have been stationed here to contribute to the common good?

People have a way of simultaneously disrespecting and flattering each other, striving to outdo one another or groveling in each other's presence.

Consider how flawed and hollow it is for someone to declare, 'I intend to treat you fairly.' There is no need for such announcements; actions will inevitably reveal the truth. Integrity should be as evident as an inscription across one's forehead. A person's true nature is immediately apparent in their gaze, just as those who are in love can read all in the eyes of their beloved. An honest and good person should be akin to someone with a strong scent; one inevitably perceives their presence as soon as they are nearby, whether one wishes to or not. Contrived simplicity, however, is like a bent stick—its deceitfulness cannot lead to anything straight. Above all, beware of the façade of friendship—nothing is more contemptible than feigned camaraderie. The virtuous, straightforward, and kind-hearted can be identified by their gaze; there is no mistaking it.

The capacity to live well resides in the soul, particularly when it is indifferent to things that are themselves indifferent. Such indifference is attained when it considers each of these things individually and collectively, understanding that they do not impose any judgement upon us, nor do they approach us on their own. These things are static; it is we who form judgements about them. It is within our power to refrain from solidifying these judgements within ourselves, or, should they have subtly crept into our minds, to eradicate them. Remember, our time to practice this is fleeting, as life itself is short. Moreover, what burden lies in doing so? If such matters are natural, we should welcome them, for they will then align with our own nature and be easy for us. But if they are against nature, we should seek what is compatible with our own nature and pursue that, even if it doesn't bring fame. Every individual has the right to pursue their own welfare.

Reflect on the origin of each event, what it's composed of, what it will transform into, and what it will be like after it has transformed, understanding that it will experience no true harm.

If someone has wronged you, first consider your relationship with humanity, recognizing that we are created to coexist; and from another perspective, some of us are positioned to lead, like a ram leads sheep or a bull leads a herd. Start from fundamental principles: if the universe is more than mere atoms, then nature orchestrates everything. If this is the case, the lesser is meant for the sake of the greater, and these in turn for each other.

Second, think about the nature of people in their daily lives—how they behave at the table, in private, and what beliefs compel them. Consider the arrogance with which they often act.

Third, realize that if people act appropriately, there's no cause for displeasure. But if they act inappropriately, it is clear they do so without intention or knowledge. Since every soul is averse to being stripped of truth, so too is it averse to being deprived of the ability to treat everyone justly. Consequently, individuals feel aggrieved when they are labeled as unjust, ungrateful, greedy, and generally as wrongdoers to others.

Fourth, acknowledge that you too are prone to err, as you are human like everyone else. Even if you avoid certain mistakes, the propensity to make them remains—perhaps restrained by fear or a desire to protect your reputation or some other base motive.

Fifth, realize that it is often hard to judge whether actions are wrong, as context is key. Truly understanding another's actions requires much learning and insight.

Sixth, when you are deeply upset or saddened, remind yourself that life is fleeting; we all soon reach life's end.

Seventh, remember that it is not the actions of others that upset us; they act according to their own principles. It is our reactions—our opinions—that cause distress. Remove these judgments as if they were a source of pain, and your anger will dissipate. To do this, consider that another person's misdeeds do not tarnish your character, unless being dishonored is the only evil. Otherwise, you too must be at fault in many ways.

Eighth, reflect on how anger and annoyance cause more suffering than the deeds that provoke them.

Ninth, understand that true goodness is unconquerable if it is sincere and not just a facade. No matter how aggressive someone may be, they cannot harm you if you maintain a kind demeanor towards them. When correcting them, do so gently and not to reproach but to help, without bitterness, and not for show, but in genuine concern for their well-being.

Remember these nine rules as gifts from the Muses, and let them guide you in becoming truly human in your life. You must avoid both flattery and resentment towards others, as both are antisocial and lead to harm. Keep in mind, especially when anger tries to take hold, that succumbing to passion is not befitting a man. True manliness is found in gentleness and kindness, which align more closely with human nature and represent real strength and resilience—not the tendency to give in to fits of passion and dissatisfaction. A man's mind, when free from the influence of passions, is strongest. Pain is a sign of weakness, as is anger, for both indicate a surrender to one's wounds.

Accept a tenth gift from Apollo, the leader of the Muses: expecting bad people not to commit wrongs is folly—it is wishing for the impossible. But it's both irrational and tyrannical to permit such behavior towards others while expecting to be exempt yourself.

Be vigilant against four significant misjudgments of your higher faculties. When you spot them, eradicate them with these reminders: "This thought is unnecessary; this undermines community; this statement isn't a reflection of my true beliefs." It's absurd to speak anything other than your truth. And finally, when you find yourself self-critical, recognize it as your divine part being suppressed by the inferior, mortal parts—the body and its crude pleasures.

Your body's elemental parts—those aligned with air and fire that should naturally rise, and those of earth and water that should fall—are constrained within you according to the universe's order. They remain fixed where they are, despite their natural inclinations, until the universe signals their release. Isn't it peculiar that your rational part, which faces no such coercion and is meant to act according to its nature, is the one that resists and becomes discontent? Any movement towards injustice, excess, anger, sorrow, or fear is a deviation from its nature. Furthermore, when your innermost intelligence bristles against the unfolding of events, it too abandons its duty, which includes not only fairness but also reverence and respect for the divine, as these are part of living in harmony with the world's order and actually take precedence over mere acts of justice.

A person without a consistent purpose in life cannot remain consistent throughout their life. But it's not sufficient to have any purpose; it should be one aligned with the common good and community welfare. A person who dedicates their efforts to such a shared purpose will act consistently across all aspects of life, maintaining their integrity.

Contemplate the difference between the rural and urban mouse and the dread and panic of the city-dweller.

Socrates likened popular opinion to mythical monsters designed to scare children.

At their events, the Spartans would offer shaded seating to their guests but would sit themselves in any available spot, indifferent to comfort.

Socrates excused himself from visiting Perdiccas, explaining that he did not wish to suffer the worst kind of downfall, which for him meant accepting a favor without the ability to return it.

The ancient Ephesians advised keeping the memory of virtuous men from the past constantly in mind.

The Pythagoreans encouraged us to observe the sky each morning, to remind ourselves of the celestial bodies that consistently follow the same paths and duties, reflecting on their perpetual order and unadorned beauty, as no star is hidden behind a veil.

Reflect upon the kind of man Socrates was when he donned an animal skin after his wife, Xanthippe, took his cloak and left, and consider his response to friends who felt embarrassed and withdrew from him due to his appearance.

You cannot expect to prescribe rules for others in writing or teaching unless you have first mastered following rules yourself. This is even more applicable to life.

Remember that you are a servant; the liberty of free speech is not yours.
And with that thought, my heart filled with mirth.
They will curse virtue itself with harsh words.
Seeking a fig in the midst of winter is the folly of a madman, akin to longing for a lost child when it is no longer possible to have one.

When a person embraces their child, Epictetus suggested they should whisper to themselves that the child may die tomorrow. When told that such words were of bad omen, Epictetus countered by saying that no natural process should be considered ill-omened; if so, even talking about the harvesting of grain could be seen as such.

The green grape, the ripe cluster, the dried raisin—all are mere transformations, not into nonexistence, but into a state not yet realized.

No one can deprive us of our free will.
Epictetus also taught that we should develop a method for how we agree or disagree with things, ensuring our actions are appropriate to the situation, aligned with communal benefit, and reflective of the true worth of what's at stake. He advised a complete detachment from sensual desires and to avoid displaying aversion toward anything beyond our control.

The argument, he pointed out, is not trivial; it's about whether one is sane or not.

Socrates questioned, "What do you desire? The souls of rational beings or of irrational ones?" When the answer was rational beings, and specifically those who are sound of mind, he then queried why they were not sought after. Given the response that such souls are already possessed, Socrates then challenged, why then is there conflict and disagreement?

Workbook Exercises
Book XI

Living with Wisdom

Think about the role of wisdom in your daily life. Reflect on a decision you made recently. Did you apply wisdom, and if not, what would a wiser approach have looked like?

The Power of Choice

Consider Marcus' emphasis on the power of choice in shaping our lives. Reflect on a recent choice you made. Were you fully aware of its power at the moment, and how might you exercise this power more deliberately?

Being True to Oneself

Consider how you can be true to yourself in all situations. Reflect on a time when external pressure made you act contrary to your values. How can you ensure that you remain true to yourself in the future?

Meditations: Book XII

E verything you strive for by a roundabout path is available to you now, if you do not
deny it to yourself. This means ignoring all that has passed, entrusting the future
to the divine, and shaping the present in harmony with devotion and righteousness. In
devotion, find satisfaction with your allotted place in the world, for nature has tailored it
for you and you for it. In righteousness, speak the truth openly and act in accordance with
the laws and the true value of things. Do not let the wrongdoing of others, public opinion,
or the desires of the body distract you; leave such concerns to those who are swayed by
them. When the time comes for you to leave this life, if you have honored your rational
nature and the divinity within you, fearing not that you must stop living but rather that
you may have never started living in accord with nature, you will be a person worthy of
the universe that gave you birth. You will no longer feel alien in your own world, nor will
you be amazed by daily occurrences as if they were unexpected, nor dependent on external
things.

God perceives the essence of all human minds, stripped of their bodily shells and all
impurities. He engages only with the intellect that has emanated from his own divine
essence into these vessels. If you practice seeing yourself in this light, you will shed much
of your distress. For the person who pays no heed to the flesh that clothes him will
hardly concern himself with clothing, shelter, reputation, or other outward trappings and
displays.

You are made of three components: a small body, a little breath (life), and intelligence.
The first two are yours in the sense that you are responsible for their care, but the
third—your intelligence—is truly yours. Thus, if you detach from your consciousness all
that others say or do, all that you yourself have said or done, all that troubles you about
the future, all that clings to you by nature through the body and the life force within it

against your will, and all that the whirling currents of the external world bring about, so that your rational power, unhampered by fate, can live purely and freely on its own, doing what is right, accepting what happens, and speaking the truth—if, I say, you disentangle this guiding part of yourself from the sensory impressions, from past and future events, and mold yourself in the image of Empedocles' sphere:

"Completely round, in blissful solitude reposing;"

and if you concentrate on living the life that is truly yours—that is, the present—then you will be able to spend the remainder of your life up until death free from disturbances, in a noble manner, in tune with your own spirit (the divinity within you).

I have often marveled at how everyone values themselves more than anyone else, yet they place less value on their own opinion of themselves than on the opinions of others. If a god or a wise teacher appeared and instructed a person to conceal nothing in his thoughts, to plan nothing that he wouldn't declare the moment it came to mind, he would be unable to bear this directive even for a single day. Such is the weight we give to our neighbors' thoughts about us over what we think of ourselves.

How can it be that the gods, after arranging all things well and with kindness toward humankind, neglected this one aspect: that some very good men, those who have engaged deeply with the divine through acts of piety and devout practices, should cease to exist entirely after death, never to live again?

Yet, if this is indeed the case, be convinced that had it been proper for things to be otherwise, the gods would have made it so. For if it were just, it would also be within the realm of possibility; and if it were natural, nature would have allowed it. Therefore, if they do not exist after death, be assured that it was not meant to be. We find ourselves questioning the gods on this matter, which we would only do if we believed them to be supremely good and just. But if they are just, they would not have neglected anything in the universe, allowing it to be unfair or irrational.

Train yourself even in tasks you believe impossible. For instance, the left hand, typically unskilled in most activities due to lack of practice, can hold the reins more firmly than the right when trained to do so.

Reflect on the state a person should be in, both in body and soul, when death arrives; ponder the brevity of life, the vast expanse of time before and after, the fragility of all matter.

Consider the essential nature of things stripped of their outward appearance; the true ends of actions; understand the nature of pain, pleasure, death, and reputation; realize who is the source of his own discomfort; that no one can impede another; and that all is a matter of perception.

In applying your principles, behave more like a wrestler than a gladiator. A gladiator puts down his weapon and is defeated, but a wrestler uses nothing but his own body and only needs to employ it rightly.

Inspect things closely to see what they truly are, breaking them down into their material, form, and purpose.

Consider the power you have to do nothing but what aligns with divine will, and to accept all that the divine bestows.

Regarding events that unfold according to nature, we should not fault the gods, for they commit no wrongs either willingly or unwillingly, nor humans, for they err only unwillingly. Hence, we should find no fault with anyone.

How odd and out of place is the person who is astonished by anything that occurs in life.

Whether there is a destiny that is unchangeable and an all-encompassing order, or a providential guidance in the universe, or a chaos devoid of purpose and director, consider your response accordingly. If an unchangeable fate governs all, why do you struggle against it? If a providential power exists and can be appealed to, then endeavor to align yourself with the divine will. If chaos reigns, take solace in possessing your own governing intelligence amidst the storm. And if you are swept away, let it be only your body and breath that are taken, for your inner rationality remains untouched.

Does a lamp's light retain its glow without dimming until it is snuffed out? Similarly, should not the truth within you, and your commitment to justice and moderation, endure until your life's end?

When someone appears to have committed a wrongdoing, ask yourself: How can I be certain that this act is unjust? Even if the person has done wrong, isn't it possible they have already judged themselves harshly? To expect the impossible, such as a bad person never doing wrong, is as unreasonable as expecting a fig tree not to produce sap in its fruit or babies not to cry. If someone is of a particular disposition, what else can they do? If you find yourself easily annoyed, work to change this in yourself.

If an action is not just, refrain from doing it; if a statement is not true, refrain from saying it. In all things, examine the nature of what seems real to you, dissecting it into its essence, its matter, its intent, and the time it has to exist.

Recognize that within you lies something superior and more divine than the emotions which tug at you. What now occupies my thoughts—is it fear, doubt, desire, or something similar?

Firstly, act neither rashly nor without purpose. Secondly, let your actions aim for nothing other than the common good.

Remember that soon you will be gone, and nowhere to be found; the same goes for all that you see now and all who live now. Nature is designed for transformation, to allow the new to take the place of the old.

Keep in mind that all things are a matter of perspective, which you control. Remove your judgments whenever you choose, and like a sailor who rounds a cape, you will find tranquility, stability, and a serene harbor.

Any action, whatever it may be, upon completion at its appropriate time, incurs no harm by ending; nor does the individual performing it incur any harm because the action has ended. Similarly, our life, which is a compilation of many such actions, when it concludes at the right moment, experiences no harm due to its conclusion; nor is the individual who concludes this sequence at the proper time mistreated. Nature sets the appropriate time and limit for this—sometimes as with old age, which is unique to the individual, but always in line with the universal nature. It is this change within its parts that keeps the entire universe forever fresh and flawless. And everything that benefits the whole is invariably good and timely. Therefore, the end of life for any person is not evil, for it is neither dishonorable—being beyond personal control and not contrary to the collective well-being—nor is it detrimental, but rather appropriate, beneficial, and in harmony with the universal order. In this way, one is aligned with the divine, moving in accordance with it and with the same objectives in mind.

You should be prepared with these three principles: In your actions, do nothing without consideration or in a way that deviates from what justice would dictate. In regard to external events that befall you, recognize they are the result of either randomness or divine providence, and neither fault randomness nor reproach providence. Secondly, reflect on the nature of every entity from its inception to the infusion of life, and from the infusion to its departure, and understand the composition and dissolution of each being. Thirdly, if you were to be lifted above the earth and gaze upon human affairs from that height, noticing the vast diversity yet the brevity of it all, as well as seeing the multitudes that inhabit the skies and the ether, remember that from such a vantage point, you would witness the same patterns over and over—the consistent forms and fleeting existence. Can such observations be a source of pride?

Dismiss your preconceptions and you are liberated. What then prevents you from letting them go?

Whenever you are disturbed by anything, you have forgotten that all happens in accordance with the nature of the universe; you have forgotten that other people's wrong-doings are not your concern; you have forgotten that everything occurs as it has always occurred, and will continue to do so, and is happening thus throughout the world. You have overlooked the profound relationship that exists between an individual and all of humanity – it is not a connection of mere blood or seed, but of the mind. You have overlooked that the mind of every person is divine and is a stream flowing from the divine; you have overlooked that nothing truly belongs to anyone, for even one's child, one's body, and even one's very soul are gifts from the divine; you have overlooked that all is a matter of perspective; and lastly, you have forgotten that every person lives only in the present moment, and loses only this.

Regularly remind yourself of those who have felt deeply aggrieved, those who have achieved great renown or suffered misfortune, or have become enemies or fortunes of any magnitude: ponder where they all are now. They are but smoke, dust, and legend – or not even a legend. And remember also those who have lived a certain way – Fabius Catullinus in the countryside, Lucius Lupus in his gardens, Stertinius at Baiae, Tiberius in Capri, Velius Rufus at Velia – and reflect on the fervor with which they sought after things tied to pride; and how trivial are the things for which men labor with such vehemence; and how much more philosophical it is for a person to make use of the chances at hand in a way that is fitting of a rational and social being.

Workbook Exercises
Book XII

Alignment with the Universe

Marcus often speaks about aligning individual actions with the nature of the universe. Reflect on your personal goals. How do they align with the broader workings of the world around you?

Detachment from Materialism

Contemplate Marcus' view on detachment from material possessions. Reflect on your relationship with material goods. How might a Stoic perspective alter your view of what's truly valuable?

Individual Purpose

Consider Marcus' thoughts on living with purpose. Reflect on what 'living purposefully' means to you. Are there changes you can make to lead a more purpose-driven life?

Printed in Great Britain
by Amazon

37234209R00086